RETURN

MW01492820

RETURNING THE LOST SHEEP

Ministry to the Alcoholic and Addict:
An Orthodox Perspective

FATHER DIMITRIOS MORAITIS

Printed in the United States of America
ISBN: 978-0-9895764-0-6

Front and Back Cover Art: Byzantine Iconography, in watercolor, by Maria Athanasiou

Typeface: Times New Roman.

Front Cover Design: Father Louis Nicholas

Back Cover Design: Father Dimitrios Moraitis

Website: www.returningthelostsheep.com

Acknowledgments

I wish to thank everyone who helped me prepare this book, from its infancy as a doctoral project, to this last edit. These wonderful people include: Father Joseph Allen, the director of my doctoral program and first reader of my dissertation, Doctor Andrew Purvis, Doctor George Demacopoulos, Jon Varlamos, Dorothy Athanas, and Tim Kokonas. The artwork by Maria Athanasiou vividly captured the sacrificial essence of ministry that I strove to communicate in this book. Special thanks goes to Father Samaras who spent the most time and effort helping mold the doctoral project into a book; Father Maximos Constas for his insightful comments and for directing me to fabulous patristic and contemporary sources, which enhanced this project theologically.

I also wish to thank the staff at the Hazelden Recovery Center in Center City, Minnesota, for the training I received in ministry to the addict's family, as well as Michael Massari and Carol Parks from the Saint Francis Recovery Community in Fort Lauderdale, Florida, for their suggestions in the clinical field, and for allowing me to briefly serve as a spiritual director of their recovery community.

My dear cousin, Dr. Chris Kyriakides, has been a constant support in my ministry, in myriad ways, including helping to underwrite the cost of the publication of this book, and its free distribution to all active Greek Orthodox Priests in the United States. I am grateful to him and his family.

I am indebted to the communities I have served as a priest, including Saint Demetrios in Chicago, Illinois, Saints Constantine and Helen in Fayetteville, North Carolina, and Saint Paraskevi in Greenlawn, New York. I say I'm indebted because of the many parishioners who invited me into their life stories so I might bring Christ's Love and healing to their hearts, as imperfect as I am. I also thank Father Louis Nicholas for helping me co-pastor and allowing me some liberties to edit this book.

I am eternally grateful for the care that I received from my spiritual father, Reverend Dr. Chris Metropulos, who has guided me from my initial call to ministry, until the present time. I could not have asked for a better role model.

His Eminence, Metropolitan Gerasimos of San Francisco, was an example to me during my studies at Holy Cross Greek Orthodox Theological School. As a member of the clergy and a therapist, he showed, through his teaching as a professor, and in his interaction with the students as the Director of Student Life, that it was not only possible, but important, that clergy serve not only as priests, but as pastoral counselors. His forward to this book is an honor and a blessing.

I would not be the priest or the man that I am without the love and support of my family. Therefore I want to thank my wife, Presvytera Flora and my daughters, Arsenia and Chrisoula, who endured many days, weeks, and even months of my absence, sometimes physically, sometimes emotionally, so I could minister to alcoholics and addicts, and for this book to become a reality.

Finally, but most importantly, I want to thank my Lord and Savior Jesus Christ for the first and second gift of life that He gave me, and for the perfect example of ministry that He left us in the Gospels.

Contents

Forward

Returning the Lost Sheep: Ministry to the Alcoholic and Addict: An Orthodox Perspective by the Reverend Dimitrios Moraitis is a comprehensive coverage of addiction, in general, and of alcoholism, in particular.

Moraitis traces the root causes of alcoholism and offers an analysis within a patristic and spiritual context. Hence, although the production of neurotransmitters, as dopamine, is cited as an impetus for the alcoholic to persist in the addiction, the persistence itself is better understood in scriptural and patristic terms as "sin," recognizing that "the theological understanding of alcoholism is so diverse that 'it seems probable that failure on the part of many ministers to find adequate answers to this question is one important reason why organized religion has not made a larger contribution to the solution of the problem.'"

And, yet, in his experience, "recovery for many alcoholics would not be possible without the ability [of alcoholics] to forgive themselves." Redemption and the process of "working out one's salvation" can be valid, operative categories in recovery efforts. Moraitis presents numerous possibilities to religious workers to be of assistance in these efforts. He advocates the creation of networks within religious communities, in general, and in Orthodox Christian communities, in particular. At the very least, Father Moraitis hopes "his study will spark conversations about the way in which clergy should minister to alcoholics and addicts."

Given that statistics cited by the Centers for Disease Control and Prevention, for example, indicate an excess of 51% regular usage of alcohol by adults 18 years of age and over (study conducted in 2011), resulting in 25,692 alcohol-related deaths (excluding accidents or homicides), *Returning the Lost Sheep* is, in my opinion, a significant contribution in understanding addiction, that can benefit the clergy. I will highly recommend its study by my own clergy. The work, replete with a substantial bibliography, constitutes a compelling argument, as well as a timely opportunity, for the involvement of clergy and other religious workers in our ongoing efforts to seek integration or, particularly for the addict, reintegration, into the church community.

—*His Eminence, Metropolitan Gerasimos of San Francisco*

RETURNING THE LOST SHEEP

Part One

What is Alcoholism?

There is a Problem

Alcoholism is a primary, chronic disease with genetic, psychological, and environmental factors influencing its development and manifestations. Often progressive and fatal, the disease is characterized by continuous and periodic impaired control over drinking, preoccupation with the drug alcohol, use of alcohol despite adverse consequences, and distortions in thinking, most notably denial.[1] Since alcoholism and drug addiction are both illnesses that deal with the abuse of mind-altering substances, and since their physical and spiritual symptoms are similar, as well the processes used for recovery, whenever the word "alcohol" is used it can be substituted for the word "drugs" and vice-versa.

Orthodox priests are generally unprepared to minister to alcoholics and addicts, partly because there is insufficient training for seminarians and clergy concerning ministry to alcoholics and addicts—at best a one-hour class is provided within the context of their pastoral theological training. Furthermore, there is a lack of written material (from an Orthodox perspective), concerning recovery. The first two books written by Orthodox writers on the topic of recovery from alcoholism and addiction were only recently published. They were very informative, yet, neither one directly addressed the role of clergy in the recovery processes. From the moment I entered the seminary, it was evident to me that there was a lack preparation with regard to how priests should minister to alcoholics and addicts. I was blessed during my spiritual journey to have volunteered as an evening manager and small group facilitator for recovering alcoholics in a half-way-house, while studying to become a social worker. Thus, as a result of my studies, my practicum and my life experiences, I

---

1   This definition was prepared by the joint commission to study the definition and criteria for the diagnosis of alcoholism of the National Council on Alcoholism and Drug Dependence and the American Society of Addiction Medicine. It was approved by the Board of Directors of NCADD on 3 February, 1990 and the Board of Directors of ASAM on 25 February, 1990.

have a unique insight into the life, recovery, and issues faced by people who are afflicted with the disease of addiction.

While still at seminary, I led several retreats on the pitfalls of alcohol and drugs. As many priests learned of my knowledge of the subject, they began to ask specific questions concerning addiction and recovery, and even referred parishioners to me in the hope I might be able to assist them in their process of getting sober. After I was ordained and assigned to a parish in Chicago, several priests immediately referred parishioners to me who were struggling with alcohol and/or drugs. The same thing happened when I transferred to North Carolina, and then later to New York. Orthodox parish priests are confronted with a plethora of ministries, some within the Church and others outside the Church. There are many demands on today's clergy. Between sacramental, administrative, and ministerial responsibilities, the priest is hard-pressed to find time to minister effectively to persons with such problems, and to be "all things to all people" (1Cor. 9:22) and at all times. Thus, a parish priest often needs to pick and choose which ministries he can offer, and how much time he can commit to those specific ministries.

Helping alcoholics and addicts is a difficult ministry. It is difficult because it is a ministry that often has few rewards due to the high rate of relapse, and comes with great frustration brought about from the resistance and denial of many alcoholics and addicts. Moreover, we fight many ethnic Orthodox cultures of secrecy, which hinders outsiders from knowing when someone has an alcohol or drug problem. Yet, the priest has a privileged position of trust in the Orthodox community. He is often the only person with whom Orthodox Christians feel comfortable to share their deepest, darkest secrets such as their son's or daughter's drinking problem. Since the Orthodox priest might be the first and only line of defense, he must be prepared to minister properly.

Priests must be involved with the processes of recovery especially since about ten percent of Americans suffer from alcoholism or addiction. Unfortunately, the surveys that I conducted in this area show that most Orthodox priests, at best, either refer parishioners in active addiction to a treatment center, or to other parishioners who they know have gotten clean and sober. Often, this is where the priest's involvement ends. This is unfortunate, especially since almost every pastoral care book instructs clergy to be part of the whole process of recovery.

Formal treatment is not the only way people change. The factors which have the greatest effect on whether an alcoholic and addict stays sober revolves around their lifestyle and social support, which includes their work, family stability, friends, the support system around them, the way they deal with stress and anger, and how they occupy their free time. Stable spiritual/religious activity also improves the chances of someone staying sober. Again, it is not enough to simply get the alcoholic and addict into treatment. The priest still plays a pivotal role after formal treatment ends by helping the alcoholic and addict to connect to the community and empowering them to use their gifts, thereby assisting with their self-esteem and self-worth. This will increase the likelihood they will stay clean and sober.

Saving the Lost Sheep

Why should we minister to alcoholics and addicts? Since God called us into ministry, He has also placed those many souls in our care. We as shepherds are called to emulate His ministry, one of perfect love and complete sacrifice (Jn 15:13). If He as the good shepherd lifts up the example of the shepherd who leaves the ninety-nine sheep to search for the lost one (Lk 15:3-7), then that is exactly what He calls us to do with the person in crisis, especially the alcoholic and addict. Furthermore, Christ reminds us that *those who are well have no need of a physician, only those who are ill* (Mt 9:12). Celebrating the Liturgy and performing the sacraments do not fulfill all the responsibilities of a priest. A priest's mission is to go out and find the sick and suffering, especially those who have been placed under his care, and to bring healing to them.

As a result of the Orthodox clergy's absence in the life of the alcoholic and addict, many Orthodox parishioners are not being referred to treatment centers for initial treatment. Furthermore, for those who are in the process of recovery, few priests ever become part of their process of recovery and, consequently, these alcoholics and addicts in recovery do not participate in the sacramental life of the Church. Whether a priest struggles with the stigma of alcoholism and addiction, the inability to commit the necessary time, or may have had a bad experience with alcohol, either personal or familial, every priest will benefit by following the directions on ministry to the alcoholic and addict found in the appendix of this book.

Of course, there are still some priests who have questions about Alcoholics Anonymous and their 12 Steps of Recovery. In Father Meletios Webber's book, *Steps of Transformation: An Orthodox Priest Explores the Twelve Steps*, the author shows that Alcoholics Anonymous and the twelve steps of recovery are consistent with Orthodox theology and tradition. In fact, in the foreword of the book, Bishop Kallistos Ware, one of the leading Orthodox theologians of our time, writes:

"Fr. Meletios provides a convincing answer to a question

that is frequently raised. Can an Orthodox Christian, it is asked, while still remaining loyal to the Church, at the same time turn for help in AA? Should we not rather put our trust in the Sacraments of Confession, Anointing (*Euchelaion*), and Holy Communion, and in the counsel and prayers of our spiritual fathers? Why seek help elsewhere? Does this signify a lack of faith? To this, Fr. Meletios replies—and I agree with him – that membership in the AA in no way contradicts or undermines membership in the Church. Quite simply, the two are not rivals, not in competition; for AA makes no claim to be a church or a religion. The Twelve Steps, as Fr. Meletios emphasizes, "will never replace the Gospels as the call of Christ." The meetings of AA are not in any sense a substitute for participation in the sacramental worship of the Church. Membership in AA will not make us less Orthodox, or less Catholic, or less whatever else we are. What AA can do – what, indeed, it has actually done for innumerable believing Christians – is to enable them to live out their faith and to experience the power of the Sacraments in a way that they had not otherwise found possible. For again and again this has been the experience of the many thousands, if not millions, who have turned to AA: *it works*. Its distinctive blend of spirituality and practicality has proven remarkably successful in the contemporary world."[2]

If Bishop Kallistos Ware, one of the leading Orthodox theologians in the world today, does not see AA as a threat to Orthodoxy, neither should we. One of the most widely used books in pastoral counseling, and a required text for most seminarians, including Orthodox seminarians, is the *Clinical Handbook of Pastoral Counseling Volumes 1&2*. In the chapter entitled "Alcohol and Other Drug Dependencies," James E. Royce gives several reasons why priests and even pastoral counselors are hesitant to minister to alcoholics and addicts.

Most pastoral counselors today possess good counseling skills, yet even these tend to shy away from problems involving

---

2   Meletios Webber, *Steps of Transformation: An Orthodox Priest Explores the Twelve Steps* (Ben Lomond: Conciliar Press, 2003), 7.

alcohol and other drugs. The reasons for this vary. One is the stereotype of the alcoholic as a skid-row bum, in spite of widespread knowledge that these constitute only three percent of alcoholics. The other ninety-seven percent are women and men representing a cross-section of parishioners: rich and poor, old and young, devout or inattentive to religion. One is tempted to think of a drug addict as a "dope fiend" you would not allow in your living room; yet when we say "drugs" we mean prescription drugs like Valium or diet pills or sleeping medications every bit as much as we mean street drugs like heroin or PCP or cocaine.[3]

James Royce also states that clergy and pastoral counselors generally do not minister to alcoholics and addicts because of the misgivings that result from their seminary training, where priests are not given adequate preparation in the area of addiction and alcoholism. In fact, eighty-five percent of seminarians felt that their seminary training was lacking in this area.[4] Other reasons why clergy do not pursue this ministry include the myth that alcoholics and addicts are hopeless or incurable; fear of getting caught up in the middle of family fights; and the fact that addiction is a complex problem requiring a professional, interdisciplinary approach. This necessitates cooperating with several other agencies and professions, whom the priest might not know how to deal with effectively. Priests need adequate preparations to overcome these obstacles. This is all the more important when we realize that many people in trouble go to their pastor first. If we take the often-quoted figure from the old Midtown Manhattan Study (Srole, 1962) that forty-two percent of problems are seen first by the clergy, the distressing fact is that only three percent of admissions to alcoholism treatment centers come from referral by clergy. Does the other thirty-nine percent represent lost parishioners?[5]

Stephen P. Apthorp is an Episcopal minister who wrote

---

3   Robert J. Wicks, et al., eds., *Clinical Handbook of Pastoral Counseling Volume 1* (Mahwah: Paulist Press, 1993), 502.

4   Ibid., 502.

5   Ibid., 502-3.

one of the first clerical handbooks for ministry to alcoholics and addicts back in 1985. Ironically, he struggled with helping addicted persons at the outset of his ministry.

"Just as ignorance of the law is no excuse, neither was my dislike of drunks and druggies a valid reason to perpetuate my disregard. By my refusal to become involved, by my reluctance to learn about alcoholism and drug abuse, by my insistence of judging drunks and druggies as deserving of their problems and by my unwillingness to respond to the suffering of family members, I was not only denying the problem of alcohol and drug abuse but contributing to it! Not to decide was to decide. My discomfort suggested I needed to care. My guilt proclaimed that God was calling me to care. But I answered God's call with indignation and complaint. Why me, Lord, why me?"[6]

Perhaps this is a question we Orthodox clergy often ask ourselves when overwhelmed by the demands on our time. Looking at all the material written on the topic of pastoral ministry, one will find similar comments from most authors. Therefore, it is not only Orthodox clergy who struggle with this ministry, but clergy in general. It is to be regretted that a faith tradition as rich as Orthodox Christianity, which emphasizes the transforming power of God, the ability for someone to repent, be transfigured and truly born again, oftentimes does not take a more active role in facilitating this transformation. We do not have to be experts in treating addictions, but we do need to be true to our calling. As priests and spiritual leaders, we need to act as channels of Christ's love and healing to our parishioners. To do this, we need some tools that will assist us in this specific ministry.

---

6   Stephen P. Apthorp, *Alcohol and Substance Abuse: A Clergy Handbook* (Wilton: Morehouse-Barlow, 1985), 4.

Statistics

What might be most surprising to clergy today is the statistical information concerning alcohol and drugs. In a national Gallup poll in 1978, one out of four families in the United States said alcohol was causing problems in their families. The poll also asked where or to whom they would turn to for help if someone in their family had a drinking problem. Incredibly, twenty-five percent said that they would turn to some kind of religious resource. Only Alcoholics Anonymous was listed more often as a source of help.[7]

The following year, a four-page questionnaire went out to four thousand Presbyterians, both clergy and laity. It was the first such survey of its kind sent to "Church people" concerning alcohol. Forty-four percent of the laity and seventy-two percent of the clergy said that the consumption of alcoholic beverages was a problem in their community. When asked if the abuse of alcohol was a problem with which the Church should become involved, forty-six percent of the laity replied affirmatively, and remarkably eighty-three percent of the clergy also replied affirmatively. Yet, when the survey asked if their congregations are currently involved with programs which involve the issue of alcohol abuse, eighty-one percent of the laity said "no," and seventy-six percent of the clergy agreed with them.[8] This showed a stark contrast between the perceived ministerial need and what ministry was actually taking place. When asked why this contrast existed, seventy-five percent responded that other programs in their community had a higher priority. Finally, sixty-nine percent of all clergy polled said that they saw no one, or no more than three alcohol-related cases in the last year.[9] This conflicts with the statistic that twenty-five percent of the people would turn to a member of the clergy if a problem with alcohol arose.

---

7   Ibid., 5.
8   Ibid., 5.
9   Ibid., 6.

In a more recent Gallup poll (1999), thirty percent of Americans admitted that drinking has been a cause of trouble in their homes. This is twice the amount recorded in 1950, and the highest statistic ever recorded in this regard.[10] The people polled also overwhelmingly believe that God can help with their problems. In another recent Gallup poll, eighty-five percent of people believe that God or some form of Higher Power performs miracles, even today; whereas only eleven percent feel that God is not involved in their lives at all. Furthermore, forty-one percent claim to have experienced a miraculous event, a physical or emotional healing, a healing in a broken relationship, or a shining act of forgiveness.[11] There is an obvious connection between brokenness and people's desire to become whole through God's help. Even George H. Gallup, Jr., the co-chair of the Gallup organization, which sponsors the Gallup poll, believes that churches can and should help with alcohol abuse. "Religious faith can play a major role not only in recovery but in prevention. Religion gives young people what they need most to combat alcohol and other drug addictions: a reason to say no."[12]

In a two-year study by the National Center of Addiction and Substance Abuse at Columbia University entitled *So Help Me God: Substance Abuse, Religion and Spirituality* completed in November of 2001, researchers sought to find out the connection between religion, spirituality and their effects on recovery from substance abuse. Below are some of their key findings.

God, religion, and spirituality are key factors for many in prevention and treatment of substance abuse and in continuing recovery.

Adults who do not consider religious beliefs important are more than one and one-half times likelier to use alcohol and cigarettes, more than three times likelier to binge drink, almost four times likelier to use an illicit drug other than marijuana and more than six times likelier to use marijuana than adults who strongly believe that religion is important.

10   Oliver J. Morgan and Merle Jordan, eds. *Addiction and Spirituality: A Multidisciplinary Approach* (Saint Louis: Chalice Press, 1999), xi.

11   Ibid.

12   Ibid., xii.

Adults who never attend religious services are almost twice as likely to drink, three times likelier to smoke, more than five times likelier to have used an illicit drug other than marijuana, almost seven times likelier to binge drink and almost eight times likelier to use marijuana than those who attend religious services at least weekly.

Teens who never attend religious services are twice as likely to drink, more than twice as likely to smoke, more than three times likelier to use marijuana and binge drink and almost four times likelier to use illicit drugs than teens who attend religious services at least weekly.

Children who strongly believe that religion is important report learning more about the risks of drugs. When discussing drugs with their parents, sixty-three percent of teens who strongly believe religion is important feel they learn a lot about the risks of drugs; only forty-one percent who believe religion is not important feel they learn a lot.

College students with no religious affiliation report higher levels of drinking and binge drinking than those of either Catholic or Protestant religious affiliation.

Ninety-four percent of clergy members—priests, ministers and rabbis—recognize substance abuse as an important issue among family members in their congregations and almost thirty-eight percent believe that alcohol abuse is involved in half or more of the family problems they confront.

Only twelve percent of clergy completed any coursework related to substance abuse while studying to be a member of the clergy and only twenty-six percent of presidents of schools of theology and seminaries report that individuals preparing for the ministry are required to take courses on this subject.

Only thirty-six percent of clergy report that they preach a sermon on substance abuse more than one a year; twenty-two percent say they never preached on the subject.

Individuals who attend spiritually-based support programs, such as 12-Step programs of Alcoholics Anonymous or Narcotics Anonymous in addition to receiving treatment are more likely to attain sobriety. Individuals in successful recovery often show greater levels of faith and spirituality than individuals who relapse.[13]

The study concludes by pointing out that, despite these facts, spirituality and religion are often overlooked as relevant factors in preventing and treating substance abuse and addiction. The study also presents suggestions for clergy taking advantage of additional substance abuse training; preaching about substance abuse issues, informally including messages about the problem throughout the organization's programs, and reaching out to treatment programs to offer spiritual support to individuals who desire such assistance.[14]

The following are some current (as of 2013), statistics on alcoholism and addiction:

There are more deaths and disabilities each year in the U.S. from substance abuse than from any other cause.

About eighteen million Americans have alcohol problems; about five to six million Americans have drug problems.

More than half of all adults have a family history of alcoholism or problem drinking.

One-quarter of all emergency room admissions, one-third of all suicides, and more than half of all homicides and incidents of domestic violence are alcohol-related.

Heavy drinking contributes to illness in each of the top three causes of death: heart disease, cancer and stroke.

Almost half of all traffic fatalities are alcohol-related.

Fetal alcohol syndrome is the leading known cause of mental retardation.

An alcoholic will negatively impact the lives of four or five other Americans (such as associates, family, and friends) while under the influence of alcohol.

---

13   National Center of Addiction and Substance Abuse at Columbia University, *So Help Me God: Substance Abuse, Religion and Spirituality*, November 2001, 2-3.
14   Ibid., 3-4.

More than eighteen percent of Americans experience alcohol abuse or alcohol dependence at some time in their lives.

Treatment for alcoholism has been shown to reduce criminal activity up to eighty percent among chronic offenders, has increased their rate of employment, decreases homelessness, and reduces all health care costs.

Children of alcoholics are significantly more likely to engage in underage alcohol use and to develop addiction and other alcohol-use disorders.

Ninety-five percent of alcoholics die from their disease and die approximately twenty-six years earlier than their normal life expectancy.

More than 700,000 Americans receive alcoholism treatment on any given day.

In the United States, 500 million work days are lost each year to alcoholism.[15]

Finally, I want to note the disturbing statistic that eighty-five percent of alcoholics and addicts never receive any treatment! With all the success stories of alcoholics and addicts that were sick, lost, dying and finally found sobriety, it is troubling that so many more are dying without even having a chance to get well. Alcoholism and drug addiction are major problems in our society, with which all clergy must be involved, especially since the recovery is based on spiritual principles.

---

15   Statistics are from the National Council on Alcoholism and Drug Dependencies (website:www.ncadd.org).

Orthodox Statistics

Through conversations with other priests and through the referrals and interventions that I was involved in throughout the country, I realized that alcoholics and addicts were not receiving adequate assistance from their clergy. To find out how much or how little ministry was taking place, I recently polled approximately ten percent of all priests actively involved in parish ministry in the Greek Orthodox Archdiocese of America. I also polled a sampling of hundreds of alcoholics and addicts in recovery during the same period of time. Here are the pertinent results:

Seventy-six percent surveyed said that alcoholism is a disease, while twenty-four percent said that it could be controlled by will power.

Two-thirds of the clergy knew the approximate number of recovering alcoholics/addicts in their parish; the same number of clergy knew the number suspected of having an alcohol/drug problem.

Thirty-eight percent of Orthodox clergy refer active alcoholics and addicts to members of the community who are in recovery, while sixty-two percent do not.

Seventy-seven percent of clergy knew of local facilities available for treatment/detoxification, yet only forty-one percent of Orthodox priests have ever referred a parishioner to a treatment center. Of those who knew, only eighteen percent of them knew where they were able obtain financial assistance for treatment.

Only twenty-three percent of Orthodox clergy have been involved with the process of the twelve steps of recovery with their parishioners in recovery. Yet, of those who had been involved, ninety-three percent said that it was a positive experience.

About half of the Orthodox clergy polled said they have heard a confession from someone in recovery, but only thirteen percent of them have ever heard a fifth step—the confession aspect of the twelve steps. Most alcoholics do their fifth step with their sponsor instead of a member of the clergy.

Only one-quarter of Orthodox clergy have ever preached a sermon dedicated to the topic of alcoholism and drug addiction.

Perhaps what is most disturbing is that last statistic in which only about one-quarter of Orthodox clergy has ever preached a sermon dedicated to the topic of alcoholism and drug addiction. How can parishioners feel they can come to the priest with issues of addiction when they have never heard the priest mention the subject in any of his sermons?

The second questionnaire was given to recovering alcoholics at AA meetings. The goal of the survey was to discover the relationship between AA and organized religion, and between clergy and recovering alcoholics and addicts. The questions addressed were: How do alcoholics view the Church in general?; does their participation in the Church decrease after they get sober?; do they substitute AA for Church services; and do they see their priest as their spiritual advisor? The questionnaire also looked at the frequency of relapse and the use of treatment centers in getting sober. The answer to these questions should disturb the clergy and those involved in the Church.

Seventy-five percent of those in recovery who were polled said they went through a substance abuse treatment program.

The average amount of times in a treatment center was more than three.

Eighty percent admitted to having relapsed at least once.

Of those who had relapsed, the average amount of relapses was fifteen.

When asked who has helped them return to sobriety, forty-three percent said AA, twenty-six percent said their sponsor, fourteen percent said a member of their family, seven percent said they did it by themselves, three percent said their minister, one percent said their work, and six percent said that it was someone or something else that helped them return to sobriety.

Over ninety percent of those polled stated that they were connected to a religious community sometime before they became active alcoholics and addicts. However, only forty-three percent stated that they currently have a religious affiliation.

Almost half of recovering addicts admitted they substituted AA for Church.

When asked what the role of their minister was in active addiction, seventy-eight percent of churchgoers said their minister did nothing to help them, nine percent said their minister helped them minimally, and thirteen percent said their minister was helpful while they actively struggled with their addictions.

When asked what the role of their minister was in getting sober, seventy-six percent of churchgoers said their minister did nothing to help them, five percent said their minister helped them minimally, and nineteen percent said their minister was helpful in getting sober.

When asked what the present role of their minister was in recovery, seventy-four percent said their minister is not involved in their recovery, four percent said their minister is minimally involved and twenty-one percent said that their minister is currently helpful.

Eighty-six percent of those polled say they have a sponsor; fourteen percent say they do not.

Amazingly, sixty-one percent report that their sponsor is their spiritual advisor, while only nineteen percent claim that their spiritual advisor is their minister.

When asked if they have ever heard their minister give a sermon on the topic of alcohol or drug abuse, ninety percent said that they have never heard a single sermon on the topic, and ten percent said that they heard one or more sermons.

Two things are evident in this survey. First, there is a disconnect between the ministry that clergy think they are offering to alcoholics and addicts, and what actual ministry is taking place. Second, when a member of the clergy is not involved in the process of recovery, chances are that the recovering person will not return to their church. It seems that Alcoholics Anonymous provides a sense of fellowship and spiritual edification for recovering alcoholics and addicts, resulting in people in recovery feeling that there is no need to reconnect with their past faith communities.

Recovering alcoholics are three times more likely to see their AA sponsor as their spiritual advisor than their priest. Of those who claim that their minister was helpful in getting them sober, over eighty percent stated that they are still connected to their faith community. This statistic alone verifies that when a member of the clergy is active in the process of recovery, alcoholics and addicts are more likely to continue or renew their participation in the Church. This is important because recovery from addiction is more of a spiritual exercise than anything else, and people in recovery are generally on a wonderful spiritual journey that can be enhanced by the priest and the Church community, and the recovering person can also enhance the Church community.

Part Two

The Cause of Alcoholism and Addiction:
A Theological Perspective

The Fall of Adam and its Consequences

Alcoholism, drug addiction and disease in general are byproducts of the Fall. They are the outcome of humanity's disconnection from God, and symptoms of life lived in a fallen world. Obviously, this separation between God and humanity was not part of God's initial plan. In the beginning, and out of God's overflowing love, He created the heavens and the earth and everything on the earth and on the sixth day He created the crown of His creation, humanity, in His image and likeness (Gen 1:27). They were given free will, because love presupposes freedom. God created man and woman as an expression of His overflowing love, and He desired that they love Him back. We all know the story of how Adam and Eve ate from the fruit of the tree of the knowledge of good and evil and as a result they were cast out of paradise.

"God set Adam and Eve in his own paradise, and laid upon them a single prohibition. If they guarded the grace and retained the loveliness of their original innocence, then the life in paradise should be theirs, without sorrow, pain, or care, and after it, the assurance of immortality in heaven. But if they went astray and became vile, throwing away their birthright of beauty, then they would come under the natural law of death and live no longer in paradise, but dying outside of it, continue in death and in corruption."[16]

Having been expelled, Adam and Eve ceased to remain in the same state as when God had created them. Moreover, they began the process of complete corruption, especially since they were under the dominion of death. As Adam and Eve began their new lives with the knowledge of good and evil, the reality of sin permeated their very existence. Genesis demonstrates the state of their corruption. Abel is murdered by the hand of his brother Cain, and wickedness infiltrates the world to such a point that even God was sorry that He had made man on earth (Gen. 6:6).

---

16   Saint Athanasios, *On the Incarnation*, (Crestwood: Saint Vladimir's Orthodox Seminary Press, 1993), 28-29.

Alcoholism, drug addiction, and illness in general are byproducts of the Fall. In the same way that Adam wanted to be god without God by eating of the fruit, the alcoholic and addict seeks substitutes for God, placing themselves, or their drug of choice, in the place of God. The addict's actions and insatiable thirst for drugs are indicative of the passions. The passions represent the lowest level of human nature. They bring humanity to a place of passivity and slavery. They overcome the will, so that those imprisoned by them are no longer people of will, but ruled, enslaved and carried along by the passions. They produce an unquenchable thirst, which seeks to be quenched, but can never be quenched.[17] The passions are the desires of the flesh that only satisfy the flesh and generally do not benefit the soul. They distract us from seeking godly things, and turn our attention and energy towards carnal or hedonistic pleasures. The passions were created as a result of man's fall, and are the driving force behind any and every addiction.

Our abuse of the gift of free will leads to many other abuses including alcoholism and drug addiction. The AMA (American Medical Association) classified alcoholism as a "disease" over fifty years ago, and it is a fact that certain people may be predisposed to excessive compulsive behaviors such as alcoholism and drug addiction. However, the primary cause of alcoholism and addiction is spiritual, and that is the reason the 12-step programs are comprised of a strong spiritual component.

---

17   Dimitru Staniloae, *Orthodox Spirituality*, (South Canaan: St. Tikhon's Seminary Press, 2003), 77.

Orthodox Christian Understanding of Illness

Historically, the Orthodox Christian Church, and Orthodox theology in general, hold the belief that there is an interconnection between soul and body, and as a result, between spiritual condition and physical illness. When we abuse our free will and violate moral laws, physical repercussions often follow. For instance, a person who overeats or who does not exercise regularly is susceptible to health problems such as high cholesterol or heart disease. Someone who is gluttonous is likely to end up obese. One who engages in sexual activities with multiple partners increases his/her chances of contracting sexually-transmitted diseases. Smokers increase their chances of getting emphysema. Even the onset of cancer is often triggered by an imbalance in the lifestyle or diet of an individual.

Conversely, many physical illnesses lead to spiritual maladies, such as anger, frustration, agony, depression, and fear. These feelings often challenge one's faith and trust in the Lord. Therefore, as clergy, we have a tremendous opportunity to minister to those who are spiritually ill, and we can combat this condition through grace, prayer and spiritual direction. Our goal is to inspire the ill person to rid himself of sins through awareness and repentance, and to renew his relationship with God.

"Those who are well have no need
of a physician,
but those who are sick."

—*Matthew 9:12*

Anyone who has ever ministered to the ill, especially to those in the hospital, understands the tremendous opportunity at hand. A healthy person can easily forget his/her mortality and dependency on God. However, once one loses their health and is humbled by major physical ailments, one is reminded of the frailty of life and of their dependency on God. Therein lies the tremendous opportunity for ministry to take place.

Like many alcoholics and addicts who struggle with their ego, I once counseled a baptized Orthodox Christian in hospice care who, in a similar fashion, struggled with his faith in God. Week after week I visited him, hoping that he would come to believe in Christ, only to be disappointed. Fortunately, he always asked me to come back the following week. Two days before his death, I asked him "You are about to die, do you believe in Jesus Christ?" He replied, "If I don't believe now, I am in big trouble." He made a profession of faith, stating that he believed that Jesus Christ is the Son of God and that He rose from the dead and brought salvation to mankind. I heard his confession and gave him Holy Communion. On the following day, as he was dying, he asked his sister why there were so many people around his bed with beards and vestments praying and kneeling. She replied that there was nobody else in the room except for her. He fell asleep in the Lord the following hour. I visited him countless times and was unable to bring him to faith, only when he was at death's doorstep, did he recognize his true mortality and dependency on God.

Concerning the relationship between man's physical and spiritual being, as well as the healing that comes through the faith of the sick person, the editor of *The Priest's Service Book* for Greek Orthodox clergy writes:

"As a result of this renewed feeling of wholeness, forgiveness and freedom from sin, the malady is either cured in its spiritual aspect through the sacramental effect of grace and, in its physical aspect through the use of the physical means of the medical sciences, OR, if the malady remains uncured, there develops in the sick person the patience, strength and courage to endure and, through full confidence, trust and love for God, to be led to a peaceful and Christian end to his/her earthly life."[18]

---

18   Evagoras Constantinides, *The Priest's Service Book*, (Merryville: Evagoras Constantinides, 1989), 157.

Whether the malady is physically cured, or patience is given to endure it, healing takes place. The link between faith and healing is obvious in Scripture. In the Old Testament, God seems to be at once the cause and the healer of the illness: "Disease and sickness come from the hand of God, as do all the fortunes and circumstance of life."[19] Unfortunately, this understanding of a punishing God "of fire and brimstone," is the image that many alcoholics have, or at least report having when they enter treatment.[20] The proof that God is not the author of evil, and the link between faith and healing, is most evident in the New Testament. In many of Jesus' healings, He tells those physically restored to "go and sin no more, your faith has made you well." It was the ill person's faith, the belief that Christ could heal the infirmity, which our Lord lifted up.

Fr. Joseph Allen, an Orthodox Christian pastoral theologian, writes that:

"The fundamental task for the pastor is still one of faith, which meets and interprets the events of life. Thus, when the physical dimension *is* involved, our prayer must be not only for healing in the narrow sense, but also for finding *meaning* in that physical disease; this is true even though we pray and anoint for a *cure* of the ailment. In short, whether or not a physical cure comes, we still pray for and anoint the person."[21]

Illness is often the only way that we face the ultimate issues of life. The struggles we have inside, including any hate, revenge, and anger, which are sometimes fostered in our relationships with others, are seen in a new light when we experience a personal illness. It is during these moments that we not only focus on the big picture, but also the finality of the big picture, and become willing to reconcile with others thereby beginning our reconciliation with God. Somatically, a recovery

---

19   Joseph J. Allen, ed. *Orthodox Synthesis: The Unity of Theological Thought*, (Crestwood: Saint Vladimir's Seminary Press, 1981), 215.

20   Countless testimonies in AA meetings support this misunderstanding of God.

21   Ibid., 218-19.

from illness can reflect the goodness of God.[22]

The role of the clergy in healing, and the connection between physical and spiritual illness, are best seen in two passages of the New Testament. In the Gospel of Mark, Jesus calls His twelve disciples and gives them authority to teach and to heal. "*So they went out and proclaimed that all should repent. They cast out many demons, and anointed with oil many who were sick and cured them*" (Mark 6:12-13). And, in the universal letter of Saint James, we read:

Are any among you suffering? They should pray. Are any cheerful? They should sing songs of praise. Are any among you sick? They should call for the elders of the church and have them pray over them, anointing them with oil in the name of the Lord. The prayer of faith will save the sick, and the Lord will raise them up; and anyone who has committed sins will be forgiven. Therefore confess your sins to one another, and pray for one another, so that you may be healed. The prayer of the righteous is powerful and effective. (James 5:13-16)

It is clear in Scripture that there is an interrelation between spiritual and physical illness, and that clergy have been given the authority and the call to heal both the physical and spiritual. Christ not only healed the sick and inspired the souls of many, but He also cast out demons, restoring to normalcy those who were once not in their right minds.

Alcoholism is a disease that affects the mind, body and spirit. In the case of the alcoholic and addict, both the body and the soul are in need of healing. When an alcoholic or addict stops using, he/she will begin the process of physical healing. But mere physical healing will not bring about personal wholeness. Personal wholeness has to do with one regaining a sense of his/ her relationship with God. This relationship can be restored, but only through the healing of the soul. Being sober is not merely the absence of mind-altering substances. Rather, it is the ability to think and act correctly. Spiritual sobriety, also known in the Orthodox Christian world as "nepsis," is a state

---

22   Ibid., 220.

of watchfulness or sobriety that comes as a result of catharsis—usually attributed with monasticism. Monks go through a period of testing and preparation while they are novices, then they are tonsured monks by the abbot of the monastery when he feels they are spiritually ready. This spiritual readiness takes place through their participation in the services, sacraments, and most importantly, their relationship with their spiritual father. Similarly, through AA, and especially working the twelve steps of the program geared to address and correct spiritual maladies, the recovering addict can also participate in nepsis. Thus, through the process of getting "sober," as opposed to merely not drinking and drugging, both the body and soul receive healing.

Hierotheos Vlachos, the Metropolitan of Nafpaktos in Greece, has written profoundly on the illness and cure of the soul. In his book *Orthodox Psychotherapy: The Science of the Fathers*, he shows how Christian theology is primarily a therapeutic science. He uses the philosophical and biblical term "nous" to describe a person's mind, reason or thought—the ability to discern what is true or real. Therapy of the soul essentially means therapy and freeing of the "nous." Human nature becomes sick through its fall from God. This sickness is manifested primarily in the captivity and fall of the "nous." Adam's original sin resulted in lost divine grace, and in the blindness, darkness, and death of the "nous." Every person has experienced the fall of his noetic power (the power of the nous) to varying degrees, as each person is exposed to an environment in which this power is either not functioning or is below par. Malfunctioning of the noetic power results in bad relations between both man and God and between people. [23]

Metropolitan Hierotheos proposes that "right faith" must be emphasized if the soul is to be cured. For if the faith is distorted, then the cure is distorted. He claims that theology

---

23   Metropolitan of Nafpaktos, Hierotheos, *Orthodox Psychotherapy: The Science of the Fathers*, Esther Williams, trans. (Levadia: Birth of the Theotokos Monastery, 1994.) 36-37.

should be interpreted as medicinal; therefore, if medical science has the healthy person in mind when it tries to guide the sick person to health by various therapeutic methods, then the same can be said about theology. Theology is not only the teaching of the Church about spiritual health, but also the very path which we sick must follow in order to be healed. That is why we Orthodox give great weight to keeping our doctrines intact, not only because we fear the impairment of a teaching, but because we could lose the possibility of a cure and therefore of salvation.[24]

Before any cure can take place, it is imperative to realize that we are sick. If we do not realize we are sick, we are not likely to go to a doctor for healing. The Fathers of the Church called this "self-knowledge." Today we call it "self-awareness." Saint Maximos the Confessor, a seventh-century Father of the Church writes: "The person who has come to know the weakness of human nature has gained experience of divine power."[25]

Since most Christians in general, and alcoholics and addicts in particular, are disconnected and unaware of their spiritual conditions, those who are caught up in the disease of addiction are unable to clearly discern how to heal the "nous" and return to proper spiritual and physical health. The priest must act as therapist, guiding the sick to proper health.

A reordering of their "self-image" is necessary. It is the role of the priest or pastor to help ill people, especially alcoholics and addicts, to see who they truly are in relation to God. For example, God is our Father and we are His children, and thus brothers and sisters to each other. God made us in His image and likeness. Jesus is His Son and our God, but also our Savior. He died on the Cross for each one of us.

---

24   Ibid. 42-43.
25   Ibid. 43.

Communicating this reality is one of our primary purposes as clergy. To lose this capacity is to lose everything! The pastor cannot afford to neglect this important task of healing. In a sense, he introduces the person to himself.[26]

Ministry is inherently risky, especially to alcoholics and addicts in this day and age. Before the alcoholic receives any benefit from a priest, the priest must make a decision to become involved and minister.

---

26   Joseph J. Allen, ed. *Orthodox Synthesis: The Unity of Theological Thought*, (Crestwood: Saint Vladimir's Seminary Press, 1981), 222.

Ministry to the Alcoholic and Addict
as an Act of Compassion

If Christ's earthly ministry were to be labeled in today's terms, it would be called a compassionate outreach, a teaching and healing ministry. Christ's compassion is accurately understood as an active compassion, not a mere "feeling sorry" for the state of humanity, but a co-suffering together with it. He first restores us through Holy Baptism, and through God's grand economy, eventually fully restores us to the spiritual state that He originally planned for us. For some, the restoration is immediate and swift as we see in many of Jesus' healings. For the rest of humanity, the suffering of our bodies purifies our souls, thereby producing spiritual gifts. In Orthodox theology, this state of spiritual perfection in humanity is called *theosis*.

Dr. Andrew Purves, in his book *The Search for Compassion: Spirituality and Ministry*, focuses on the compassion of Christ, the effect it had on those whom He touched, and how Christ's compassion should be a model of ministry, which all clergy should follow. He believes that compassion is deeply rooted in the life of God as revealed to us in Jesus of Nazareth. It reveals the inner nature of God, in that we have a companion in Him, always being beside us during our most difficult times. Compassionate living is a result of this relationship and is manifested through God's continuing compassion for the world. Compassion does not call for an abstract, free-floating spirituality, and it certainly does not impose an impossible moral imperative. Rather, it is a way of living in Christ and through Christ in ministry to the suffering world. [27]

The healing of the leper (Mk 1:40-45); the healing of the epileptic youth (Mk 9:14-29), the feeding stories (Mk 6:30, 8:1-10 and the parallels); the healing of the two blind men (Mt 20:29-34); the raising of the son of the widow of Nain (Lk 7:11-17); and a summary of the ministry of Jesus (Mt 9:35-38), all

---

27   Andrew Purves, *The Search for Compassion: Spirituality and Ministry* (Louisville: Westminster/John Knox Press, 1989), 12.

demonstrate how the practice of compassion is at the core of true ministry. Dr. Purves also explores three other passages which he characterizes as "Compassion in the Teaching of Jesus"— the parables of the Unforgiving Servant (Mt 18:23-35), where one servant is forgiven an astronomical debt, but was unwilling to forgive his fellow servant a small one; the Good Samaritan (Lk 10:30-37), where the Jewish clergy were unwilling to help a half-dead Jew, but the Samaritan, treated like a second class citizen by the Jews, took the injured Jew, brought him to an Inn, and cared for him with tremendous compassion; and the Prodigal Son (Lk 15:11-32), where the father shows the ultimate and public act of forgiveness to a son who squandered the family wealth, while at the same time ministering to his unforgiving brother.[28]

These examples of compassion in Jesus' actions towards the sick and suffering and His storytelling are models for our ministry. Alcoholics and addicts need our spiritual care and compassion.

---

28   Ibid.

Who is the Alcoholic?

The alcoholic and addict is an ill person who has lost his or her way, and is similar to other people who are sick and struggling with other vices. The difference lies in the destruction that addiction causes, both physically and spiritually, to the individual and to his or her family. The center of the active alcoholic or addict's life ceases to be God, and now becomes their drug of choice, whether it is alcohol, prescription drugs, illegal drugs, or any other substance or behavior. For the addicted person, the special place in his or her heart and soul, the void which is meant to be filled by only God Himself, is now being filled with alcohol and or drugs. Sometimes the addict tries to find other pleasures to fill that void—sex, food, gambling, etc., only never to be satisfied. Gerald May, the author of *Addiction and Grace: Love and Spirituality in the Healing of Addictions,* explains it this way:

"I am convinced that all human beings have an inborn desire for God. Whether we are consciously religious or not, this desire is our deepest longing and our most precious treasure. It gives us meaning. Some of us have repressed this desire, burying it beneath so many other interests that we are completely unaware of it. Or we may experience it in different ways—as a longing for wholeness, completion, or fulfillment. Regardless of how we describe it, it is a longing for love. It is a hunger to love, to be loved, and to move closer to the Source of love. This yearning is the essence of the human spirit; it is the origin of our highest hopes and most noble dreams....Our addictions are our worst enemies. They enslave us with chains that are of our own making and yet that, paradoxically, are virtually beyond our control. Addiction also makes idolaters of us all, because it forces us to worship these objects of attachment, thereby preventing us from truly, freely loving God and one another."[29]

29   Gerald May, *Addiction and Grace: Love and Spiritu-ality in the Healing of Addictions* (New York: Harper Collins, 1988), 1-4.

Without a doubt, the drink and the drug replace God for the alcoholic and addict. The reality of God becomes distorted. The addict and the family lose touch with their souls and get lost in their addiction, or reacting to it. What was once a large circle of family and friends is now reduced to several people who are struggling with the same hell. Their world centers around **when** and **how** they are going to get their next drink or drug. The behavior of the active alcoholic and addict reflects much of what Saint Paul writes in his Epistle to the Romans (1:18-32), as he describes the origin of vice and how Christians ultimately face the wrath reserved for the unrighteous unless they change— because to turn away from God **is** to experience His wrath. The Fathers of the Church have written much on the topic of desire, God, and idolatry. Saint Maximos the Confessor says that we have an infinite desiring capacity, in the face of which nothing finite can ever satisfy us. In some ways, alcoholics and addicts have ceased to be children of God, children of light, and have become self-destructive tools of the Evil One.

Disease or Sin

As previously discussed, alcoholism has been characterized as a medical disease. Two thousand years ago, the Greek historian Plutarch said, "Drunks beget Drunkards." Plutarch was right. There is a genetic predisposition to alcoholism. Scientists in Denmark found that sons of alcoholics were about four times more likely to become alcoholics than sons of non-alcoholics.[30] This is not to say that being raised in the stress and turbulence of an alcoholic home and environment in general does not play a pivotal role in someone becoming alcoholic. Nevertheless, there exists overwhelming evidence that an imbalance in some of the chemical levels in the brain, especially dopamine, causes some people to be more susceptible to compulsive and addictive behaviors such as alcoholism and drug addiction. Simply put, dopamine is a substance that creates natural highs, and its function is to stimulate people to do things that are necessary for survival. Dopamine is released in the brain after a hard workout, great food and even after sex, and is experienced as euphoria.

Unfortunately, for some people, alcohol tricks the reward system into producing dopamine, resulting in the alcoholic feeling a state of euphoria when he or she gets drunk. After a while, alcohol takes over the reward process, controlling the production of dopamine, and not allowing it to be released in proper proportion during or after other healthy activities. As the production of dopamine tapers off over time, it forces people to drink more to achieve the same euphoric high.[31]

And yet today, the leaders in the field of alcoholism still struggle to convince many in society that alcoholism is a disease. In James R. Milam and Katherine Ketchum's book *Under the Influence*, the authors expose this common misconception:

"Today, the alcoholic is generally considered to be a moral degenerate who chooses a life of abasement and through

---

30   Eric Newhouse. *Alcohol: Cradle to Grave* (Center City: Hazelden, 2001), 27.

31   Ibid., 27.

lack of will power and maturity, allows himself to lose his job, his family, and his self-respect. The typical alcoholic, the myth informs us, is a person who would rather be drunk than sober, who lacks confidence and maturity, who is riddled with guilt and shame over past sins and misdeeds, yet lacks the strength of character to change his ways, and who has no guiding purpose or motivation in life. This myth is only one of many which rule the way we think about the disease and its victims."[32]

Lay people are not the only ones with these misconceptions. In his book, *Understanding and Counseling the Alcoholic*, Howard J. Clinebell, Jr. points out that not only is there a diversity of beliefs among the clergy, but there is also confusion between the relationship of sin and disease. As a result of the information gathered from 146 questionnaires returned by ministers who attended the first seven years of the Yale School of Alcohol Studies, Clinebell shows that the survey of these trained clergy falls into as many as seven theological positions. The following is his observation of each:

1.   *Alcoholism is a sin and not a sickness from start to finish.* This is the minority (about 5%) opinion. According to this view, alcoholism begins as the sin of drinking and ends as a sinful habit. The "all-sin" view errs in oversimplifying the causes of alcoholism.

2.   *Alcoholism begins as a personal sin and ends as a sickness.* One who drinks exposes himself to the dangers of becoming an alcoholic. Once the drinking has passed a certain point and is out of volitional control, it becomes a sickness. This view is limited by oversimplifying the causes, although it recognizes that in its advanced stages alcoholism is a sickness.

3.   *Alcoholism is a sickness that involves the sin of abuse.* This, the Roman Catholic view, says it is the abuse and

32   James R. Milam and Katherine Ketchum, *Under the Influence* (Seattle: Madrona Publishers, 1981), 32. Also see Stephen P. Apthorp., *Alcohol and Substance Abuse: A Clergy Handbook* (Wilton: Morehouse-Barlow, 1985), 54-55.

not the use of alcohol that constitutes the sin. It is the sin of excess. This concept does not establish responsibility in relation to the compulsion to drink, nor does it define a line beyond which a person is not responsible.

4.   *Alcoholism is a sickness caused by a combination of factors involving both sin and sickness.* This represents those ministers who see drinking as wrong but recognize the existence of etiological factors beyond the control of the individual. It holds that one is responsible for the factors that produce the "mental obsession" to drink, even though one is not responsible for having an atypical physical response to alcohol.

5.   *Alcoholism involves sin in the sense that it has destructive consequences.* The first three are nonjudgmental concepts. Here, if sin is defined as anything that harms personality, then alcoholism is certainly a sin. It is not a moral sin. If this definition of sin is accepted as legitimate, there can be no quarrel with its application.

6.   *Alcoholism is a social sin.* This view suggests that it is a sin only in the sense that it can be attributed to society, a symptom or evidence of the sinful condition of society. Whatever one's view of the alcoholic's responsibility, one can accept that "society greases the slope down which he slides."

7.   *Alcoholism involves original sin.* Alcoholism is the result of certain etiological factors, which include Man's egocentricity. There is selfishness at the very center of Man's nature that keeps him from doing that which he knows to be good. This selfishness is evident in the alcoholic as a symptom of inner conflict and insecurity. [33]

There is an obvious diversity of theological opinion concerning the relationship between alcoholism and sin. Clinebell

33   Howard J. Clinebell, *Understanding and Counseling the Alcoholic*, (New York: Council Press, 1978), 323. Also see Stephen P. Apthorp, *Alcohol and Substance Abuse: A Clergy Handbook* (Wilton: Morehouse-Barlow, 1985), 55-56.

himself felt that an accurate understanding of alcoholism should include factors in concept 5, 6, and 7 and possibly even number 4. Yet, the theological understanding of alcoholism is so diverse that "it seems probable that failure on the part of many ministers to find adequate answers to this question is one important reason why organized religion has not made a larger contribution to the solution of the problem."[34] Orthodox Christian theology would easily accept numbers 5, 6 and especially 7 in its understanding of alcoholism.

In a recent survey completed by about ten percent of all Greek Orthodox priests in America involved in parish ministry, I asked whether alcoholism is a disease, or whether it could be controlled by will power. While over seventy-five percent of the clergy polled said that alcoholism was a disease, almost twenty-five percent still felt that it could be controlled by will-power. One in every four Greek Orthodox parish priests does not believe that alcohol is a disease, even though the American Medical Association has classified it as such for the last fifty years. This clearly demonstrates that there is a tremendous need to educate priests in the Greek Orthodox Archdiocese concerning alcoholism.

Speaking of addiction as a disease can be pastorally effective for those alcoholics and addicts who see themselves as "sinners" unable to change their self-destructive behavior and "bound for hell." Many alcoholics with whom I worked with in a half-way-house felt very relieved when they were educated about the disease of alcoholism. "You mean I am not a bad person, just sick?" This realization truly gave them the opportunity to start anew, feel God's grace, and for some to be truly "born again." What they eventually find out is that true recovery from alcoholism and addiction only comes through implementing spiritual principles in their lives through the twelve steps of recovery. Yet for many, recovery would not be possible without the ability to forgive themselves for their past behavior. But before recovery can begin, a decision must be made.

---

34   Ibid., 323.

Recovery is Possible Because
Repentance is Possible

"Repent for the Kingdom of Heaven is at hand." This was the cry of Saint John the Baptist, and it also marks the beginning of Christ's ministry as recorded in the Gospel of Matthew. Awareness, acceptance, and repentance are necessary for the alcoholic to recover. In his homily on the Parable of the Sower, Saint John Chrysostom explains why the sower would plant good seeds on unfertile soil. He writes:

"It is impossible for the rock to become earth, or the wayside, not to be wayside, or the thorns, thorns, but, in reason-endowed creatures such as mankind, this is not so. In them, it is possible for the rock to change and become rich land, and for the wayside no longer to be trampled upon, nor lie open to all that pass by, but that it may be a fertile field; and the thorns may be destroyed, so that the seed may enjoy full security. For had it been impossible, this sower would have not sown."[35]

As clergy, we are surrounded by people whose hearts are like the hard wayside, almost impossible to plant any seed. We become frustrated with the time and effort spent in trying to penetrate the depth of their souls only to fail once again in touching them, changing them. And yet, with God's help and, in His time, all things are possible.

The Bible is filled with stories and personalities such as the Prodigal Son, Saul, and Peter, who had all fallen from the path of righteousness, only to repent and spend the rest of their lives glorifying God. Humanity is redeemable. All human beings have the capacity to know God, to repent from their destructive behavior and become whole again—even alcoholics and addicts. Anyone can recover from alcoholism except for those rare occasions where the alcoholic or addict has done irreversible damage to the brain. In the fifth chapter of the "Big Book" of Alcoholics Anonymous, entitled "How it Works," the earliest

35   Phillip Schaff ed., *Nicene and Post Nicene Fathers* [CD-ROM] (Albany: Ages Software, 1997), 594.

recovering alcoholics stated: "Rarely have we seen a person fail who has thoroughly followed our path."[36] Just about everybody is capable of sobriety.

Any alcoholic or addict who wishes to recover will, at one point or another, experience repentance. The initial repentance may be the day that one realizes that he or she is out of control, and has a problem. Repentance can take place the day one makes the decision to go into treatment. In cases that alcoholics and addicts are court ordered, or forced by parents to go to treatment, repentance can take place during treatment when they "come to the realization" that they are alcoholics or addicts, and that they need help. If repentance does not take place during treatment, or soon after, relapse will inevitably occur, and the alcoholic and addict will continue on his or her destructive course of life.

---

36   *Alcoholics Anonymous* (New York: Alcoholics Anony-mous World Services, 1976), 58.

The Power of Scripture

Scripture can play an integral part in the recovery of the alcoholic. In the Russian religious memoir, *The Way of a Pilgrim*, a spiritual classic, the holy pilgrim in search of true prayer meets a military officer who helps him and later tells him his story. According to the story, the officer's career was almost completely destroyed from heavy drinking, until he came into contact with the power of the Bible. He was given a copy of the Gospels by his spiritual father and told to read it without delay, every time he felt the urge to drink. Unfortunately, the officer took it, put it in his trunk and forgot about it.

One day, as he was searching for money in his trunk to buy wine, his eyes fell on the copy of the Gospels. He remembered the words of his confessor and decided to read the first chapter of the Gospel of Matthew. He did not understand it. Nevertheless, he forgot about the desire to drink that evening. When he woke up in the morning he was about to go out to buy wine but decided to read another chapter. He repeated this over and over. As the days passed, his struggle became easier and easier. As God's grace strengthened him, he began to understand more of what he read, and everyone was astonished at the change in his life. What was thought to be a chronic and incurable addiction completely disappeared through the reading of scripture and the grace of God. The man's commission was eventually restored to him. More importantly, he became a devoted and knowledgeable Christian.[37]

The power of the Word of God has transformed many from their sinful state into people of God. In fact, Scripture records many transformations, examples of repentance, and sinners who change for good. Alcoholics and addicts can only be inspired by these real life stories, and by the compassion of Christ. Scripture can truly have a profound effect in the life of

37   Theodore Stylianopoulos, *Bread for Life: Reading the Bible* (Brookline: Greek Orthodox Archdiocese of North and South America, Department of Religious Education, 1980), 27-29.

the alcoholic and addict—often bringing them to the point of desiring to stop their way of life. They read about how God answers the prayer of a desperate person. As the Psalmist writes:

> *For He commands and raises the stormy wind,*
> *Which lifts up the waves of the sea.*
> *They mount up to the heavens,*
> *They go down again to the depths;*
> *Their soul melts because of trouble.*
> *They reel to and fro, and stagger like a drunken man,*
> *And are at their wits' end.*
> *Then they cry out to the LORD in their trouble,*
> *And He brings them out of their distresses.*
> *He calms the storm,*
> *So that its waves are still.*

(Psalm 107:25-29)

Christ charged the apostles to continue His ministry. Priests, the successors of the apostles, must continue this ministry. Since recovery from alcoholism and addiction is a "hands on" process, and since alcoholism and addiction are truly spiritual illnesses, it is the priest who is in a position to play a pivotal role in the recovery process.

Scripture contains countless references concerning the dangers of alcohol including; Proverbs 20:1 and 23:21, Isaiah 5:22-23 and 28:7-8. In Proverbs 20:1 we see that alcohol is a deceiver, *Wine is a mocker, strong drink is a brawler, and whoever is led astray by it is not wise.* Proverbs 23:21 describes the reality that alcoholism destroys lives, *for the drunkard and the glutton will come to poverty, and drowsiness will clothe a man with rags.* In Isaiah 5:22-23, we are warned that alcohol corrupts. *Woe to men mighty at drinking wine, woe to men valiant for mixing intoxicating drink, who justify the wicked for a bribe, and take away justice from the righteous man!*

Scripture also shows us the possibilities of transforming one's life from sin to righteousness. In Saint Paul's Epistle to the Romans, he writes about the transformation that is possible for people who at one point struggle with sin and eventually overcome the passions. More importantly, in Romans 6:17-

23, he presents that struggle as a gift which can produce much spiritual fruit. In the same way one can go from being slaves of sin, to slaves of God, it is possible for someone crippled by addiction to be set free from those chains through recovery.

There is no life more evidently lived in the flesh than the life of an active alcoholic and/or addict. Their whole lives revolve around how they can maintain their destructive behavior. They truly live their life in the flesh, and their life in the spirit becomes so distorted that they begin to lose touch with their very souls. When an active alcoholic or addict begins his or her journey in recovery, a transformation begins which leads one from the life of the flesh, to life of the spirit. If the transformation does not begin, relapse is inevitable. The alcoholic will drink again; the addict will use drugs again. This is best exemplified in the eighth chapter of the Epistle to the Romans.

For those who live according to the flesh set their minds on the things of the flesh, but those who live according to the Spirit, the things of the Spirit...But if the Spirit of Him who raised Jesus from the dead dwells in you, He who raised Christ from the dead will also give life to your mortal bodies through His Spirit who dwells in you.

(Romans 8:5-11)

What the Church Fathers Say About Alcoholism

Saint John Chrysostom, who lived in the late fourth and early fifth centuries, was the most prolific preacher in the history of the Orthodox Christian Church. He served the Church in both Antioch and Constantinople, serving as the Archbishop of the latter. As a priest in 388 or 389, he preached a series of seven sermons on the parable of Lazarus and the rich man. Chrysostom began his first sermon on January 2nd, the day after the pagan feast of Saturnalia, which marked the beginning of the civil New Year. Saturnalia was a raucous festival filled with multiple parties, excessive drinking, loud music, dancing in the streets and even public sexual activities. It made Mardi Gras look like a children's party. This is how he began his sermon:

"Yesterday, although it was a feast day of Satan, you preferred to keep a spiritual feast, receiving our words with great good will, and spending most of the day here in church, drinking in a drunkenness of self-control, and dancing in the chorus of Paul. In this way a double benefit came to you, because you kept free of the disorderly dance of the drunkards and you reveled in well-ordered spiritual dances. You shared a drinking bowl which did not pour out strong wine but was filled with spiritual instruction. You became a flute and a lyre for the Holy Spirit. While others danced for the devil, you prepared yourselves by your occupation here to be spiritual instruments and vessels. You allowed the Holy Spirit to play on your souls and to breathe His grace into your hearts. Thus you sounded a harmonious melody to delight not only mankind but even the powers of heaven."[38]

Saint John Chrysostom never had a problem addressing the hypocritical behavior of his parishioners as well as the actions of civil leadership. Here, he praises those present in church for

---

38   Saint John Chrysostom, *On Wealth and Poverty* (Crestwood: Saint Vladimir's Orthodox Seminary Press, 1985), 19.

choosing to be there instead of outside with the revelers.

At this point, Saint John Chrysostom begins to preach on the importance of all people to minister to "the drunkards," even if they do not listen:

"Therefore, today, let's guard ourselves from the life of the drunkard. Let us not judge them, but free them from the shame of drinking. Let us not make fun of them, but correct them. Let us not expel them, but remove them from their drunken procession, and snatch them away from the grasp of the devil. The person who is drunk eats and drinks under the tyranny of the devil. If the drunk person insists on continuing his drinking even after we try to help him, still we have to advise and correct him, but without judgment. In the same way that rivers and springs still flow, whether or not someone is drinking of them, the one who speaks and is not listened to, still fulfills his obligation."[39]

Chrysostom reminds his listeners that the Prophet Jeremiah was ridiculed when he warned the Jews of the bad things that would befall them. He also states that when those who are drunk enter into eating establishments, they sometimes hear the gossip from other tables criticizing them, and as a result become red in the face. If someone becomes embarrassed by their actions, it can be the beginning of salvation, for they become aware of what they are doing. For those who become more aware of what they are doing, through someone else's words, will get better. Chrysostom reminds the people that Christ came to help those who are ill, not those who are well.[40]

Saint John Chrysostom is a model clergyman for all Orthodox priests. His eloquent sermons and his pastoral example are held up from generation to generation. If Saint John Chrysostom preached about the dangers of alcohol, and the need for not only clergy, but all Christians to become involved in helping those with drinking problems, should we as clergy not take the leadership role in becoming more involved?

39   John Chrysostom, *First Sermon on the Rich Man and Lazarus*, PG: 48.

40   Ibid.

You Do Not Have To Do It By Yourself

*For in that He Himself has suffered, being tempted,
He is able to aid those who are tempted.*

—Hebrews 2: 9-18

People in recovery have a special gift that no one else in society possesses. They have the incredible ability to help others get sober. The cliché often used in the rooms of AA is *"You can't keep what you have unless you give it away."* The recovering parishioner can be a tremendously useful tool for the parish priest. In the same way that Christ understands the human condition because He was truly human, as well as truly God, and today He aids us when we struggle with sin, so a recovering alcoholic understands what it means to be an active alcoholic, but more importantly, how to get sober.

Several things are necessary when using a parishioner to help another parishioner get sober. The recovering parishioner must be willing to help and willing to compromise his or her anonymity. The parishioner in recovery is taking a risk by identifying himself/herself as a recovering person. If the person he or she is helping does not wish to get sober, they might reveal to others, in and outside of the community, that the parishioner is an alcoholic or addict. Also, the priest must continue to stay active in the process of recovery. To merely "pawn off" a parishioner to another does not fulfill the priest's responsibility.

A sponsor should not serve as a spiritual father to the recovering alcoholic, but unfortunately this does happen. Since in the life of the early recovering alcoholic there are usually few if any positive spiritual role models, the sponsor often places himself or herself in that position, sometimes on purpose, other times by default. While sponsors mean well, at times they fall into the heresy of relativism, which in truth permeates much of the twelve step programs, and other times they themselves make AA their "church" because of a past negative experiences with "organized religion." Once again, in my surveys to recovering alcoholics and addicts, ninety percent said they were churchgoers before they became active alcoholics and addicts, but only forty-three said they currently had a religious affiliation. Half surveyed admitted to have substituted AA for church. Perhaps most importantly, over three-quarters of those who were at one point or another churchgoers said that their priest/minister did nothing to help them while in active addiction or assist in the process of getting clean and sober. When the priest participates in the recovery of the alcoholic, the sponsor is free to focus on guiding the newly-recovering person in matters of staying sober, while the priest can focus on guiding him or her in spiritual matters, making sure to keep him or her connected to Church. Although, in truth, there is usually some overlap.

Relapse in Sobriety

There is an applicable story attributed to Leonardo Da Vinci's portrait of the Last Supper. In the painting, Da Vinci depicts Christ and the twelve Apostles sitting around the table in the Upper Room. But he also depicts the specific moment Judas betrays Christ. When Da Vinci began to search for models for his famous painting, he first sought to find someone who resembled Christ. After searching several months, he found a man who had a glow about him. "This is definitely a man of God," he said to himself. He asked him if he would pose for his painting and the gentleman agreed.

After Da Vinci painted the Figure of Christ, he went out looking for models to pose as the Apostles. It took him only a month to find and paint eleven of the disciples, but he was having trouble locating someone to pose for Judas. He searched far and wide, in the highways and the byways, to find someone who looked destitute enough so as to resemble the betrayer of his Lord.

Finally, two years into his search, Leonardo found the perfect model lying in a back alley. He seemed lost and destitute. Da Vinci approached this homeless person and inquired whether he would be willing to pose as Judas for his painting of the Last Supper. The person began to cry. Leonardo did not know what to make of it. He tried to console the person and assure him that he had no intention of hurting his feelings. But the homeless man said to him, "I'm not crying because you have asked me to pose as Judas; I am crying because, two years ago, you asked me to pose as Christ."

This story punctuates the reality of the frailty of sobriety—here one day, gone the other. The recovering person has the ability to transcend their sinfulness and their disease, but only if he or she makes it the primary focus of their life, one day at a time.

Unfortunately, when we look into Scripture, especially the Gospels, we will find it difficult to locate people who were transfigured and transformed—only to relapse into their old behavior. We see them change and we want to think that they live happily ever after, of course that's not always the case.

Did the blind man, the paralytic, the demon-possessed man and the harlot live righteously all the days of their lives after receiving the grace of God? We don't know. Perhaps the best two examples of people failing are the betrayals of Peter and Judas. Both Peter and Judas were directly exposed to Jesus Himself, and witnessed His many healings and teachings. Both were sent out to heal and teach themselves, but Judas betrayed and Peter denied Christ—both relapsed into their old behaviors. Both betrayed Christ, but both had an opportunity to repent. Peter chose to repent and became arguably the greatest of all the Apostles. Judas, on the other hand, chose not to repent and took his own life.

Christ knows that the way of repentance is not easy. Many of the Desert Fathers compare life and repentance to a person climbing a mountain. They climb and climb and suddenly they hit a loose rock and begin sliding down. To stop their sliding, they must first realize that they are sliding. Once the sliding has stopped, they can begin climbing again. Such is the life of the alcoholic, especially one who is newly recovering. Relapse in sobriety is a reality for the alcoholic, and one which the priest must accept without judgment and frustration, but with the hope of repentance.

For just like Da Vinci's model, if we resemble Christ, it does not mean that we are guaranteed to always look like Him. Similarly, when a person gets clean and sober, there is no guarantee that he or she will stay clean and sober. If to resemble Christ means a lifetime commitment that is practiced daily, then staying sober is also a lifetime commitment that can only be possible by working on it one day at a time.

Then Peter came to Him and said, "Lord, how often
shall my brother sin against me, and I forgive him?
Up to seven times?" Jesus said to him, "I do not say to you,
up to seven times, but up to seventy times seven.

--Matthew 18:21-23

How many of us have heard confessions from a particular
parishioner, only to hear the same sins asked to be forgiven over
and over? And how many of us in our own spiritual life struggle
with the same sins and temptations? The hope is that with every
confession, with every commitment to change a bad behavior,
the next time we are confronted with the same temptation, we
will be stronger and more prepared to resist it. If we do fall, the
hope is that it will not be as bad and as long as the last time. So
it is with the recovering alcoholic and addict. The frustration of
relapse is easily seen in the very words of Saint Paul:

I do not understand my own actions. For I do not do what
I want, but I do the very thing I hate. Now if I do what I do not
want, I agree that the law is good. But in fact it is no longer I that
do it, but sin that dwells within me. For I know that nothing good
dwells within me, that is, in my flesh. I can will what is right, but
I cannot do it. For I do not do the good I want, but the evil I do
not want is what I do. Now if I do what I do not want, it is no
longer I that do it, but sin that dwells within me. So I find it to be
a law that when I want to do what is good, evil lies close at hand.
(Rom 7:15-21)

In the mind and in the heart, the alcoholic does not want
to drink again, and the addict does not want to use again, but his
will to stay clean and sober is often overtaken by the compulsion
to drink. Relapse is a reality in the life of the alcoholic and
addict, especially very early in their sobriety. In fact, in one of
my recent surveys of alcoholics and addicts, over eighty percent
admit to having relapsed at least once. Of those who relapsed,
the average amount of times was fifteen. Priests must not feel
as if they have failed when a parishioner relapses, especially in
early recovery, but they must work intensely to help the alcoholic
return to the road of recovery.

The Twelve Steps

Since its inception over seventy-five years ago, millions of alcoholics have gotten sober through the Twelve Step program of Alcoholics Anonymous. Today, the twelve steps of recovery are still the most effective means of getting sober and staying sober. Most treatment centers use the twelve steps as the foundation of their recovery program and as a major part of aftercare. The twelve steps of Alcoholics Anonymous are scripturally-based. Since the disease of alcoholism is in part spiritual, the recovery process must also be scriptural. It is well-documented, especially in Christian-based twelve step programs, that the program of recovery is founded on spiritual principles taking in much of the New Testament, weighing heavily on Paul's letters and the Epistle of James.[41] It is a program of awareness, accountability, forgiveness, restitution, and a daily commitment to God and to staying sober. The steps reflect the Gospel, in that all of God's people are called to repentance through the grace of God and the power of the Holy Spirit.

The twelve-step program of recovery used in Alcoholics Anonymous utilizes the transforming power and the truth of the Gospel message, leading those seeking sobriety to the proper spiritual discipline. This in turn leads them to transformed lives that are lived in the spirit, and free of alcohol and drugs. They cease to be "slaves of sin" (Rom. 6:17), and instead become "slaves of righteousness" (Rom. 6:18). Through the steps, they learn that they need not live in the flesh, but in the spirit (Rom. 8:9).

---

41   Luke 6:31, Matthew 5:23, Romans 7:18, 12:1, Philippians 2:13, 1 Corinthians 10:12, Colossians 3:16, Galatians 6:1, 1 John 1:9, James 4:10, 5:14, 5:16, and Lamentations 3:40.

Orthodox Publications on Alcoholism and Addiction

Father Meletios Webber accurately describes the alcoholic and addict in his book *Steps of Transformation: An Orthodox Priest Explores the Twelve Steps*. He describes the disease of addiction and gives a glimpse of what life in Alcoholics Anonymous is like. More importantly, Father Meletios examines the twelve steps, grounds them in Orthodox theology, and shows how they can be implemented in the lives of Orthodox Christians who are, and are not addicted. His book wonderfully puts at ease the fears of Orthodox Christians who suspect the twelve steps and Alcoholics Anonymous are a cult and threat to Orthodoxy. Unfortunately, the book stops before giving practical guidelines to clergy on ministry to the addict.

In Victor Mihailoff's book, *Breaking the Chains of Addiction: How to Use Ancient Eastern Orthodox Spirituality to Free our Minds and Bodies from all Addictions*, the "former addict" uses Scripture and many of the writings of the Fathers of the Church to show how to overcome passions, sin, and addiction. Anyone who struggles with sin will benefit greatly from this book and the resources that it provides to battle temptation. This is only the second book written in English by an Orthodox Christian dealing with the topic of alcoholism and addiction. However, the book rarely discusses issues directly pertaining to the alcoholic and addict. For instance, there is a chapter entitled "Holy Communion." This is a topic of concern for those in recovery. Mihailoff rightly discusses the need for people to receive Holy Communion in order to enter the Kingdom of Heaven. He also writes about some people who do not receive because of the fear of catching a disease.

Some people are concerned that receiving the Holy Gifts from the same spoon as others exposes them to a high risk of contracting communicable diseases. This is an old question that has come up many times over the centuries. It is inconceivable that Christ would allow any disease to transmit through His Holy Blood and Flesh. There is not a single documented case of any

Orthodox Christian catching a communicable disease through receiving Holy Communion via the same spoon that had just been in the mouth of a person suffering from a highly contagious disease. Not even a deacon or a priest who consumes the remains of the chalice contents after all communicants have partaken of the Sacrament catches any communicable diseases.[42]

While this is true, it does not discuss the greatest concern of communion for most alcoholics, especially those who are in early recovery. How does someone who is in a program or recovery from alcohol addiction, a program that believes in total abstinence, receive Holy Communion which has alcohol in it? This is the major issue facing Orthodox Christians and Communion in early recovery.[43]

---

42   Victor Mihailoff. *Breaking the Chains of Addiction: How to Use Ancient Eastern Orthodox Spirituality to Free our Minds and Bodies from all Addictions*. (Salisbury: Regina Orthodox Press, 2005), 109.

43   For more information on the reception of Holy Communion by alcoholics and addicts, see the chapter, in this book, on "Reintegrating the Addict into the Life of the Church." pp 120-125.

Part Three

Twelve Things Every Priest Should Know to Properly Minister to Alcoholics and Addicts

Core Competencies for Clergy
and Other Pastoral Ministers
in Addressing Alcohol and Drug Dependence
and the Impact on Family Members.

In an Expert Consensus Panel Meeting conducted by the U.S. Department of Health and Human Services entitled *Substance Abuse and the Family: Defining the Role of the Faith Community,* Washington DC; February, 2003, a group of clergy, psychologists, and addiction specialists met in dialogue. Realizing that members of the clergy are often the first people to whom many turn in times of crisis, and understanding that clergy are rarely sufficiently trained to minister to alcoholics and addicts, this panel sought to put together a document listing the core competencies of the ministry. As a result, they produced a document entitled: *Core Competencies for Clergy and Other Pastoral Ministers in Addressing Alcohol and Drug Dependence and the Impact On Family Members.*[44] They identified these competencies as a specific guide essential to clergy and pastoral ministers in meeting the needs of persons with alcohol or drug dependence and their families. The following are the specific competencies:

1.   Be aware of the generally accepted definition of alcohol and drug dependence and the societal stigma attached to alcohol and drug dependence.

2.   Be knowledgeable about the signs of alcohol and drug dependence, the characteristics of withdrawal, the effects on the individual and the family, and the characteristics of the stages of recovery.

3.   Be aware that possible indicators of the disease

---

44   U.S. Department of Health and Human Services. Substance Abuse and Mental Health Services Administration. 2004. *Core Competencies for Clergy and Other Pastoral Ministers in Addressing Alcohol and Drug Dependence and the Impact on Family Members: Report of an Expert Consensus Panel Meeting February 26-27, 2003, Washington, DC, 13.*

may include, among others: marital conflict, family violence (physical, emotional, and verbal) suicide, hospitalization, or encounters with the criminal justice system.

4.   Understand that addiction erodes and blocks religious and spiritual development; and be able to effectively communicate the importance of spirituality and the practice of religion in recovery, using the scripture, traditions, and rituals of the faith community.

5.   Be aware of the potential benefits of early intervention to the addicted person, the family system, and the affected children.

6.   Be aware of appropriate pastoral interactions with the addicted person, the family system, and the affected children.

7.   Be able to communicate and sustain an appropriate level of concern, and messages of hope and caring.

8.   Be familiar with and utilize available community resources to ensure a continuum of care for the addicted person, the family system, and the affected children.

9.   Have a general knowledge of and, where possible, exposure to the 12-step programs - AA, NA, Al-Anon, Nar-Anon, Alateen, A.C.O.A., etc. and other groups.

10.   Be able to acknowledge and address values, issues, and attitudes regarding alcohol and drug use and dependence in oneself and one's own family.

11.   Be able to shape, form, and educate a caring congregation that welcomes and supports persons and families affected by alcohol and drug dependence.

12.   Be aware of how prevention strategies can benefit the larger community.[45]

---

45   Ibid. 13.

Core Competency 1

*Be aware of the generally accepted
definition of alcohol and drug dependence
and the societal stigma attached
to alcohol and drug dependence*

Alcoholism is a Disease
and not the Result of Moral Weakness

Alcoholism is a primary, chronic disease with genetic, psychological and environmental factors influencing its development and manifestations. The disease is often progressive and fatal. It is characterized by continuous and periodic impaired control over drinking, preoccupation with the drug alcohol, use of alcohol despite adverse consequences, and distortions in thinking, most notably denial.[46]

As mentioned earlier, not only has this been scientifically supported, but the disease concept allows the recovering people to put the past behind them and truly begin anew. Since there is a proven genetic predisposition to addictive behavior, clergy can warn families and individuals who have alcoholism in their family history to abstain or limit their consumption of alcohol. They can also educate them about healthy ways to deal with and relieve stress.

The Disease is Often Progressive and Fatal

In Alcoholics Anonymous meetings, members constantly remind each other that this disease is "cunning, baffling, and

---

46   This definition was prepared by the joint commission to study the definition and criteria for the diagnosis of alcoholism of the National Council on Alcoholism and Drug Dependence and the American Society of Addiction Medicine. It was approved by the Board of Directors of NCADD on 3 February, 1990 and the Board of Directors of ASAM on 25 February, 1990.

powerful,"[47] and that if they do not get sober they will end up in one of three places: prison, an institution, or in the grave. When untreated, alcoholism and drug addiction will destroy a person's life, and will adversely affect everyone around them. Most of the time, the progression is insidious, even to those closest to the addicted person.

Barbara S. Cole, an addiction therapist and recovering person, describes the subtle changes in this way: "Like lights dimming in indistinguishable increments, our precious attributes fade....When it happens this slowly, others can barely tell that our souls have been robbed of their light."[48] Even the closest family members miss the signs of the progression of the disease, and are unable to help. By the time they realize it, the damage caused by alcoholism and addiction becomes so painful that they withdraw from the alcoholic in confusion, pity, or disgust.[49]

---

47   *Alcoholics Anonymous* (New York: Alcoholics Anonymous World Services, 1976), 58-59.

48   James B. Nelson, *Thirst: God and the Alcoholic Experience.* (Louisville: Westminster John Knox Press, 2004), 38.

49   Ibid., 38.

It is characterized
by continuous and periodic impaired
control over drinking,
preoccupation with the drug alcohol,
and use of alcohol despite adverse consequences

Characteristics of Addiction

An alcoholic must get drunk and an addict must get high—it has become their nature, part-and-parcel of their disease. Consequently, an alcoholic and addict's life is controlled by when, where, and how they will get their next fix. During the first phases of the disease, this need is not as obvious—but as it progresses, the signs become more evident. In the beginning, an alcoholic might be sure to have "a couple of beers in the fridge" at all times, especially before they sleep. Later in the progression, alcohol must be involved in every social function they attend and, if it is not, they make sure to drink before they attend or they sneak something in with them. Finally, alcohol is stashed in various places of their house or in the office to ensure that a drink is never more than a few feet away.

Some alcoholics, however, do not fit this model. A small minority are not daily drinkers. In fact, some alcoholics might only drink once a year. However, when they drink, they frequently go on binges which can last for days. When alcohol is introduced into the bodies of these types of alcoholics, they cannot control themselves. Although the consequences of drinking are quite evident since these alcoholics drink so infrequently, it is hard to convince them that they have a problem. Ultimately, the first step in AA helps them overcome this obstacle—*"We admit that we are powerless over alcohol, and that our lives have become unmanageable."* An alcoholic and addict's life cannot remain manageable. The consequences of binge drinking or of daily drinking will eventually catch up with them, causing great pain and even greater frustration.

"Insanity is doing the same thing over and over again, but expecting different results." This is the definition heard in every AA room. "Next time it will be different," is the mantra that the alcoholic's and addict's disease tells them. "I know I passed out, or got a DWI, or got into a fight the last time that I drank, but this time it will be different." "Next time I will stick to beer only; next time I won't mix my drinks; next time I will eat before I begin my drinking." Or the most frequently-quoted line, "Next time, I won't drink as much." This is the insanity that almost all alcoholics experience. As crazy as it sounds, alcoholics must justify and rationalize their decisions to drink again: if they don't, they must come to terms with their problem. Until they come to terms with the problem, they will continue to "fool" themselves, thinking that things will be different next time. These are the beginnings of distortions of thought.

> It (Addiction) is characterized
> by distortions in thinking,
> most notably denial

Denial

Denial is the greatest obstacle to sobriety and, at the same time, it is its number one symptom. The disease of addiction is the only disease that tells those afflicted with it that they do not have a disease. The addicted person is more unable, rather than unwilling, to accept that there is a problem. Justification and rationalization control active alcoholics, allowing them to continue the destructive lifestyle without realizing and admitting that they are actually destroying themselves. Since denial in the addicted person lies mostly in the subconscious, it is referred to as "honest self-deception."[50]

Denial prevents clergy, family, friends and co-workers from helping the addicted person. It affects and erodes most relationships, since the perception exists that the addict is constantly lying to protect himself and his way of life—even though it is self-destructive. Such great denial by both the addict and his dysfunctional family invariably causes the ministering

---

50   Robert J. Wicks & Richard D. Parsons, & Donald Capps, ed. Clinical Handbook of Pastoral Counseling: Volume 1. (Mahwah: Paulist Press, 1985), 503.

priest to first confront not the cause of the denial and disease, but only the surface symptoms of the root issue. Priests normally want to reduce pain and suffering in members of their congregation. Empathy is what many desire from their priest. But in these situations, one of the worst things clergy can do is to get caught in the family's dysfunction. Both the addicted person and his or her family have become sick through years of abuse. The coping mechanisms most families use lead to other problems and emotional illnesses. A priest who empathizes with the addicted person and their family instead of confronting them may actually enable the disease.

Thus, it is easy to understand why a priest might become frustrated when his attempts to help, comfort, heal, and restore families appear disregarded by those who initially sought help. This is because families are unable to accept his ministry. In short, the whole family has become sick.[51]

---

51   Ibid., 70.

Societal stigma

Growing up in New York, I remember the homeless on the streets of downtown Manhattan, reeking of alcohol as they begged for hand-outs. This image of the down-trodden homeless alcoholic, which constitutes only about three percent of all alcoholics, is still the prevalent image for alcoholism. Likewise, one assumes that a drug addict is strung-out on heroin or crack-cocaine. The businessman with the three-martini-lunch, and the person who abuses prescribed pain-killers, such as oxycodone and vicodin, are rarely the symbols of addiction. And yet, these alcoholics and addicts greatly outnumber the others.

These societal images also prevent those who struggle with alcohol and drugs from recognizing their plight. Alcoholics sometimes compare themselves favorably to the homeless alcoholic and say, *"When I get that bad, I'll get help."* However, if they finally do accept that they are indeed alcoholics and addicts, the disease model makes the blow softer, and it is the clergy's responsibility to affirm that alcoholism and drug addiction are diseases; that the person is not bad, evil, or going to hell, but rather sick and in need of recovery.

Core Competency 2

*Be knowledgeable about the signs
of alcohol and drug dependence,
the characteristics of withdrawal,
the effects on the individual and the family,
and the characteristics of the stages of recovery.*

Categories of Drugs

It is important, as clergy, to have a general understanding of the various classifications of drugs. Whether hearing about them during youth retreats, or having them mentioned within the context of a confession, or while ministering to an alcoholic and addict, the priest should have a general knowledge of the various drugs out there, as well as their effects and withdrawal symptoms.

Depressants

Depressants are called such because they depress the way the central nervous system functions, and may even induce coma. The most popular depressant is alcohol, which is also the most abused drug in the world. Depressants include barbiturates such as *Seconal* (reds, red devils), *Nembutal* (yellows, yellow jackets), *Tuinal* (rainbows), *Amytal* (blues, blue heaven), and *Phenobarbital*. The most famous non-barbiturate sedatives are *Quaaludes* (ludes). *Benzodiazepines*, also known as minor tranquilizers, are often prescribed and include among others *Valium, Librium, Xanax, Klonopin* and the date-rape drug *Rohypnol*, known as *Roofies*. Finally, over-the-counter sleep aids such as Nytol and Sominex, as well as other cold and allergy medications contain depressant drugs. Commonly prescribed sleeping pills such as *Ambien, Restoril, and Chloral Hydrate* are also depressants and are very addictive. An overdose of depressants is extremely dangerous and can be fatal, since the fatal dosage can be as little as ten times the therapeutic dosage. Alcohol blood poisoning happens too often, especially when young people begin experimenting with alcohol, and this can cause death. Also, withdrawal from depressants can be fatal. In addition to anxiety, loss of appetite, irritability, insomnia, and seizures, severe withdrawal from alcohol can cause delirium tremens, also known as DTs. Supervised detoxification is highly recommended when an addict on depressants or, especially an alcoholic, has abruptly stopped using.

Stimulants

Stimulants increase central nervous activity. Respiration, heart rate, alertness and motor activity are heightened. Stimulants include legal drugs with minor psychoactivity, such as caffeine and nicotine. They also include more harsh drugs, such as amphetamines and meth-amphetamines. Crystal-meth is very addictive and has become a major social problem. *Ritalin* (Dexedrine) often prescribed for ADHD is a stimulant. Cocaine, and the derivative, Crack, are still the most abused stimulant, while *Benzedrine*, also known as Black Beauties or Crosstops, are still abused today. Stimulants affect the brain's reward center. They cause the body not to experience fatigue, thirst or hunger. The compulsion to use these drugs, the desire to maintain the high, and the unpleasantness of withdrawal make overdose fairly common.[52] Tremors, sweating, flushing, rapid heartbeat, insomnia, anxiety, paranoia, convulsions, heart attack and stroke are all symptoms of an overdose. Though withdrawal is not necessarily dangerous, severe symptoms such as irritability, restlessness, anxiety, and chronic headaches, can last for days and are quite unpleasant. Withdrawal from cocaine and amphetamines can last for months and include symptoms such as intense drug craving, the inability to experience pleasure, and depression.

---

52   Gary L. Fisher, & Thomas C. Harrison, Second Edition: *Substance Abuse: Information for School Counselors, Social Workers, Therapists, and Counselors.* (Needham Heights: Allyn & Bacon, 2000). P. 21

Opiates

Opiates are naturally occurring, as well as synthetically produced. They include opium, codeine, morphine, heroin, Vicodin, Dilauded, Percodan, Darvon, Demerol, Talwin, Methadone, and the oft-abused Oxycodone. Opiates are used primarily for pain management, as well as cough suppression and constipation. They induce such a euphoric feeling that many use them as recreational drugs. Methadone, a synthetic opiate, is used in the treatment of heroin addiction. It's effective because it produces a less euphoric feeling, which lasts much longer than heroin without inducing the withdrawal symptoms of heroin. An overdose of heroin is common, because it is usually injected directly into the body, purchased in unreliable strengths, and affects the brain directly: at times causing respiratory distress. Allergic reaction to heroin, or substances used to cut it can lead to cardiac arrest. Heroin and Oxycodone addicts build up a tolerance to their drugs quickly and, when used regularly, develop a rapid physical dependence. *Suboxone/Sobutex,* is an oft-used synthetic heroin prescribed by addiction professionals to wean addicts off heroin. Unfortunately, the use of this drug, which should be no longer than a few months in duration, can last for years, with the addict struggling to stop using it. Withdrawal from opiates is unpleasant and uncomfortable, but rarely results in death.

Hallucinogens

Hallucinogens are found naturally and they are also produced synthetically. They include *LCD* (acid, fry), *psilocybin* (magic mushrooms, shrooms), *morning glory seeds* (heavenly blue), *mescaline* (mesc, big chief, peyote), *ketamine* (K, Special K, Vitamin K), *STP* (serenity, tranquility, peace), *PCP* (angel dust), and the more widely-used *MDA* (ecstasy). Hallucinogens produce a state of altered consciousness. It's almost impossible to overdose with hallucinogens. While there is no physical dependency, unless mixed with other substances, psychological dependency (craving) does occur. The most common chronic effects are "flashbacks," a recurrence of the effect, even years after taking the drug.

Cannabis and Others

Marijuana is the most commonly used illegal drug. Users experience euphoria and heightened awareness. An overdose is not common, and tolerance may or may not increase. Withdrawal only occurs in high-dosage users who quit abruptly. Marijuana may serve as a gateway drug that can lead to more harsh drugs and the possibility of addiction. "Spice," a synthetic marijuana, is sold over the counter, often to minors. Though laws are being enacted to make the sale of spice illegal, the easy access to this drug makes it a danger, especially to the very young. Several states have recently legalized, or at least de-criminalized marijuana. This is problematic in that the more readily available and culturally acceptable marijuana becomes, the more likely that it will be abused.

Inhalants and Volatile hydrocarbons are chemicals, which are sometime inhaled by young people. The use of these drugs is called sniffing or "huffing." They range from any of the mineral spirits, to glues, sprays and even liquid paper. They produce euphoria, dizziness and reduced inhibition. Overuse may cause irregular heartbeats and coma from a lack of oxygen.

Used illegally by athletes to improve athletic performance and muscle mass, Anabolic Steroids are synthetic drugs, which are normally prescribed for testosterone replacement. Chronic effects include atrophy of testicles, impaired production of sperm, and infertility. There are physical and psychological withdrawal symptoms with anabolic steroids, most notably loss of muscle mass and fits of rage.

The Signs of Alcohol and Drug Dependence

How can one know if someone has a drug or alcohol problem? Most of the people I have helped were brought to my attention as referrals from family members or other clergy. Rarely will an active member of the community come to clergy and tell them that he or she has a problem, although this does happen. When this does occur, it is typically somebody you would not suspect as having a problem. More likely, the person in need of help was once active in the Church, but over time they withdrew. Alcoholics and addicts, especially those active in the Church, will withdraw because they perceive that they are involved in behavior which is less than holy and not acceptable by the Church. Sometimes, the alcoholic or addict returns to Church as a last resort and plea for help.

Clergy learn that someone has a problem with alcohol or drugs in one of four ways: they are either told about the person by a friend or other third party; they are told about the person by a member of the family; they are approached by the addicted person asking for help, or they deduce by themselves that one of their parishioners has a problem. A priest once asked me, "If one of my parish council members constantly smells of alcohol, does that mean that he is an alcoholic?" I told him it is quite possible. "How do I help him?" he asked.

When is it appropriate to confront someone about their drinking or drugging? It is one thing when a parishioner comes to a priest and asks them to help someone who has a problem and quite another thing for the priest himself, as the spiritual leader of the congregation, to approach one of his own and inquire if they have a drinking problem. Feelings can be hurt and relationships ruined. I have found that it is best to talk to the spouse first, if he or she is married, and see if everything is going well at home before approaching the alcoholic or addict. For Orthodox clergy, a visit to the house during a house blessing or holy unction service is not only a good way to assess the situation, but a great opportunity to have an open conversation with the addicted person in the comfort of their own home. This might allow the sick person to speak of things they ordinarily would not share in Church.

Whether it is a suspicion one has as a priest, or an appeal from a loved one, it is imperative that clergy meet directly with the person suspected of having a problem directly and to assess for himself if a problem does in fact exist. Perhaps, in meeting personally with the person at risk, the priest may ask pertinent questions to more clearly reveal any existence of a problem with addiction.

Questions to Help Determine Alcoholism or Addiction

Does discussion about excessive drinking annoy you?

Has anyone ever complained about your drinking?

Have you or someone else worried that you drink too much?

Have you ever cut down on your drinking or quit for a while? (Most do not realize that "going on the wagon" is not a sign of control but a symptom of alcoholism. The true social drinker does not play these games of control.)

Have you noticed that you can handle more liquor now than previously? (Again, many will boast about being able to drink more than everybody else, not realizing that elevated tolerance is a classic symptom of alcoholism rather than assurance that one is immune. Only in very late stages of the disease is there a sharp drop in tolerance.)

Do you drink more when under pressure, after a disappointment, or after a quarrel? Do you find yourself making excuses for having a drink? (A social drinker may *enjoy* a drink; the alcoholic *uses* it to cope.)

Do you sometimes drink more than you intend or promise, even though you don't get drunk? (A myth is that the alcoholic gets drunk every time he drinks. However, drinking more than one intends to is a sign that one is beginning to lose control.)

Do you think about your next drink or whether there will be enough to drink?

Do you find yourself ready for the next round of drinks ahead of the others?

Are you sometimes uncomfortable when no liquor is available?

Do you wish to continue drinking after the others have had enough?

Do you do or say things when drinking that you can't remember the next day?

Do you remember the first time you had a drink? (Most of us can't, but the alcoholic often can, and reacts with a smirk, smile or a frown.)

Do you ever enjoy an eye-opener? (a drink the morning after).

Have you ever switched types of liquor to control your drinking?

Does the availability of drink affect your choice of what you do in your recreation time?

(For spouse) Do you see a notable personality change in your spouse after they have had a few drinks?

The person who answers "yes" to two or three of the above questions is probably in the early-stages of alcoholism. Five "yes" answers would be a certain diagnosis, and indicative of at least the early-middle stages of the disease.[53] Clergy should ask these questions directly to the person suspected of alcoholism, with the pretense of "ruling out" that their parishioner is an alcoholic. If the parishioner answers yes to more than three questions, then you should let them know that they are on the verge of becoming an alcoholic. I have seen this information affect several people in profound ways, almost scaring them into not drinking again.

----

53   Wicks, Robert J. & Richard D. Parsons, & Donald Capps, eds. Clinical Handbook of Pastoral Counseling: Volume 1. (Mahwah: Paulist Press, 1985), 505-506.

Progression of the Disease

Dr. E.M. Jellinek first charted the progression of the disease of alcoholism. Using the "Jellinek Curve," three distinct stages are evident as the disease progresses: Early, Middle and Late. The elements of these stages are symptoms of the illness. Most alcoholics and addicts will not experience all of the elements of the stages, but they will experience many of them as their disease progresses.

Early Stage of Alcoholism

Alcohol is used to calm nerves

Alcohol is used as a sedative to deal with stressful situations. Instead of dealing with "life on life's terms," the alcoholic uses alcohol as a crutch, to help deal with difficult moments.

Being uncomfortable in a situation
where there is no alcohol/drugs present

In social situations or other situations where alcohol or drugs are not available, alcoholics and addicts will either sneak in their drug of choice, avoid going all together, or they may sweat it out until they can get their hands on alcohol or drugs. The person at this point has become psychologically addicted to alcohol or drugs because it has become of primary concern to them.

Increase in alcohol tolerance

Addicts in general, and alcoholics specifically, build up a tolerance to drugs over time and they need more of it to achieve the same "high." This eventually changes as the disease progresses to the later stages.

Driving while under the influence

As alcohol and drug use continues, consequences become more severe. Driving under the influence is a symptom of poor decision-making often caused by continued and dependent use of mind-altering substances. A responsible drinker will not get a DUI.

Desiring to continue drinking/using
when others have stopped

Social drinkers will drink during appropriate social settings and, when the event is over, the drinking stops. For the alcoholic, however, the drinking does not stop at the end of the social event, but continues in different settings, and might continue when the alcoholic is alone.

Relief drinking commences

When stress or problems in life arise, a person in the early stages of alcoholism will use alcohol to alleviate or forget the pain. This person also uses alcohol to overcome the consequences of earlier episodes of drinking—they drink to get over their hangovers.

Secret irritation
when individual's drinking/using is discussed

As alcohol use increases, loved ones will begin confronting the alcoholic's behavior. At this point, the alcoholic will become irritated and will internalize the anger. This anger often comes out during other conflicts.

Occasional memory lapses
after heavy drinking/using

Black-outs are the precursors to memory lapses. Black-outs are a period of time when drinking occurs, which the drinker cannot remember. During these short memory lapses, the drinker has difficulty remembering certain events from the prior evening. These might be insignificant events, or they might consist of risky behavior, which might be morally questionable or even illegal.

Preoccupation with alcohol/drugs (thinking about next drink/drug)

People in the early stages of alcoholism or addiction might start thinking during their work day about when, how, and where they will engage in their consumption of alcohol or drugs later in the day. This preoccupation with alcohol can be a "fantasy time" allowing them to cope with the stressors of work or life. The drug addict might be making arrangements to "cop" his drug of choice from his local dealer during their work day.

Lying about drinking

Denial begins to appear during this stage. The alcoholic and/or addict will deny that they are using or at least lie about the amount they are using. When the consequences of alcoholism and drug addiction begin to show, family members and loved ones usually confront the addicted person. Lying about the amount and/or frequency of use is the normal early response from someone who is on their way to addiction.

Increased frequency of relief drinking/using

As the disease continues, it also progresses. The alcoholic or addict will increase the use of their drug, not necessarily to get high, but to overcome pain, depression, or an earlier drinking or drugging binge.

Loss of Control Phase

It is possible, though not likely, to have some of these above-mentioned characteristics and still be able to stop drinking and drugging on one's own. However, there is a point of no return that every alcoholic and addict goes through. It is a line that once crossed, makes it almost impossible for the person to return to normalcy without recovery.

Rationalization begins

Rationalization is one of our higher defense mechanisms. For the alcoholic, however, it becomes one of the leading coping mechanisms. Anyone in their right mind will realize that continued use and abuse of alcohol and/or drugs will certainly lead to severe consequences, perhaps even death. Rationalization gives the addict an excuse to use (my job, wife, kids, financial situation, many failures, etc.), and to use as frequently as needed. It is the old "if you had my life, you would drink too" mentality. Rationalization is used to make the unbelievable believable. Rationalization also convinces the addict that his or her drug and alcohol use will not have the same devastating physical and emotional consequences that it does for other addicts, because he or she is different. Rationalization is only one part of the "denial system" of the alcoholic or addict. Other higher defense mechanisms include:

Projection—blaming others for consequences caused by their drinking and drugging;

Minimization—acknowledging that there might be a small problem, but constantly minimizing the problem and the consequences;

Fragmentation—inability or unwillingness to see the total reality (euphoric recall);

Intellectualizing—Removing oneself from one's feelings by using verbal abstractions. All of these are the building blocks of denial and need to be torn down so recovery can take place.

Hiding liquor/drugs, sneaking drinks/drugs

The hiding of alcohol speaks volumes to the severity of one's problem. As odd and unbelievable as this behavior seems to family members, it is part and parcel of the disease of alcoholism. When the alcoholic knows that he has alcohol "stashed away," he rests easier knowing that whatever may happen, he is only a few feet away from his next drink. Family members are in awe when they find out the places where alcohol was hidden—under the sink, in the laundry room, in the toilet bowl tank, in the basement or attic, under a floor board, or hidden inside a wall.

Meals missed due to drinking/using

Food starts becoming less of a priority to the alcoholic and addict, as many meals are consumed in liquid form. Cocaine addicts often lose weight at the height of their addiction. Even robust men can wilt away to nothing. Alcoholics will lose weight when they begin to reach rock-bottom. It's not just food that gets neglected. Other basic necessities, such as health and hygiene are neglected as well.

Middle Stage

Increasing dependence on alcohol/drugs

The alcoholic or addict begins to need his or her drug of choice more and more. Amounts consumed and frequency of use increase.

Preoccupation with drinking/drugging activities

Up to this point, contemplating when and where to enjoy their next drink and drug helped alcoholics and addicts get through work. At this stage, alcoholics and addicts become so consumed by the compulsion that their work suffers tremendously. They cannot wait to get through the day to use again.

Drinking/using bolstered with excuses

The use of alcohol/drugs intensifies and is fueled by a myriad of excuses rationalizing the increased usage.

Feeling guilty about drinking/using

Alcoholics and addicts are not heartless monsters. Rather, they are sick people who need to consume alcohol or drugs. They know that their actions hurt others, especially those closest to them, causing their loved ones pain that results in guilt. They medicate this pain with more alcohol or drugs.

Irritability when drinking/using

Some alcoholics become angry or violent when they drink. Even the most "loveable drunks" will become more and more irritable as the disease progresses, especially if something comes between them and their drink or drug.

Tremors and early morning drinks/drugs

Morning detoxification (the body's natural way of cleaning alcohol from the system) causes the "shakes" or tremors. If alcoholism continues, the alcoholic will likely soon find out that a morning "cocktail" helps to alleviate the shakes and "get him through the day."

Avoids non-drinking/non-using situations

At this stage, the alcoholic will avoid being in situations where he cannot consume alcohol or drugs. This means the possibility of cutting ties with family members by being absent from gatherings and holiday celebrations if they cannot drink or drug. Those addicted to cocaine will likely avoid social settings so they can "snort a line."

Dishonesty in non-drinking/using activities

Bad behavior expands outside of drinking and drugging. The addicted person might begin to steal things that he covets, or engage in embezzling at work, without thinking about the consequences.

Increased memory blackouts

What was once an isolated incident or two becomes more frequent. There are blocks of time which alcoholics or addicts cannot account for during their binges. They literally cannot remember what they did the night before.

Loss of other interests

Hobbies, participation in athletics, and even care for other family members become insignificant in comparison to drinking and drugging.

Unable to discuss problems

Although the addicted person knows that there is a problem, discussing it with others is seen as an admission of the problem and is therefore avoided.

Promises and resolutions fail repeatedly

Most alcoholics do not realize that "going on the wagon" is often not a sign of control but a symptom of alcoholism. After a period of abstinence, drinking will likely begin. Alcohol and drugs are merely the *symptom*, the problem is the *person*. Even if you remove alcohol or drugs, the alcoholic or addict will still exhibit behavior that is self-destructive.

Grandiose and aggressive behavior

Alcoholics are egomaniacs with inferiority complexes. In an attempt to "puff themselves up" in order to hide their low self-esteem, alcoholics will blow things out of proportion by lying or using elaborate props to show off in front of others. Behavior becomes more aggressive when using, resulting in threats and fights.

Neglect of food

What first started as skipping a meal or two has now become an increased neglect of food. Physical repercussions and ailments from not eating regularly begin to mount.

Controlled drinking/using fails

The addict's attempts to stop, either for a while or forever, continue to fail. Even efforts to drink less are unsuccessful. Once that first drink or drug enters the body of the alcoholic or addict, they are never sure when they will be able to stop.

Family, work, money problems

Problems caused by the persistent use of alcohol and/or drugs will affect all facets of the sick person's life. In addition to familial and work problems, financial problems caused by the cost of drinking and drugging, compounded by lost productivity at work, will result in tremendous financial constraints for the addict and his/her family.

Family and friends avoided; drinking/using alone (secretly)

Even the alcoholic and addict realize they are going downhill. Being around a family this deep in addiction is painful. Isolating one's self and using alone becomes the norm.

Possible job loss

Continued abuse of alcohol and/or drugs will usually result in job loss. Some will lose their jobs or businesses early in their disease, while others somehow manage to keep their jobs as their lives spiral out of control.

Late Stage

Many alcoholics and addicts never reach this advanced stage. The pain and consequences of abusing alcohol and/or drugs either leads them to do something about it, or they die before they can reach this stage. Alcoholics and addicts in this stage may start to resemble the "skid row drunk" or the "strung-out drug addict."

Radical deterioration of family relationships

The addicted person pushes everyone away, or drives them away by their behavior. The family system is now breaking down quickly.

Thinks responsibility interferes with drinking/using

Using is all that matters. Even some of the core responsibilities of life are seen as unnecessary and a nuisance. These responsibilities may include work, childcare, and even hygiene.

Loss of family

At one point or another, family members must "jump off the Titanic" before it sinks. Family members have become negatively affected as a result of living with the alcoholic/addict, and they must begin to care for themselves, even if it means the dissolution of the family. If it has not happened yet, divorce is inevitable.

Physical and oral deterioration

Physical ailments resulting from alcoholism and drug addiction are well-documented. From severe liver damage to permanent brain damage, extended use and abuse of alcohol and/or drugs results in serious physical illness and, when untreated, will lead to death. Oral difficulties such as slurred speech, the inability to communicate, and serious tooth decay are also common in the late stages of alcoholism

Unreasonable resentments

Almost all alcoholics in the late stage of their disease have unreasonable resentments. As the consequences of abusing alcohol or drugs become more severe, someone or something needs to be blamed. Rarely will the diseased person hold themselves accountable for their actions. Addicts will begin to project anger on members of their family, friends, bosses, coworkers, the bank teller, the bartender, the IRS, and any other person, or thing they can blame for their own sorry state.

Loss of willpower and onset of lengthy drunks/highs

Earlier in the disease, the alcoholic/addict could stop using for a number of days. Now it is almost impossible to stop. Alcohol/drug binges begin to last longer and the consequences of use are more severe. Conflict, brawling, and arrests increase.

Urgent need for morning drinking/drugs

The alcoholic experiences morning tremors and the shakes—the body's normal response to the poison consumed the previous evening. In an attempt to alleviate the tremors and return to their state of "normalcy," the alcoholic regularly drinks the "morning cocktail" and the addict experiences the "early morning buzz."

Geographical escape attempted

A geographical escape is an attempt to change someone's lifestyle by changing where they live. Alcoholics and addicts often try a "geographical cure," thinking that by moving to either another neighborhood, city or state, the change of scenery will help them combat their illness. Unfortunately, wherever they go, their illness goes with them. Alcoholics and addicts can change **where** they live, but unless they change **who** they are, they will drink or drug again.

Persistent remorse

The feeling of guilt and remorse for their actions during a drunken stupor, and the reality that they are slowly killing themselves, are indications that the alcoholic and/or addict is in the late stage of alcoholism/addiction.

Impaired thinking and memory loss

Even the most intelligent person will suffer impaired thinking and memory loss as a result of continued abuse of alcohol/drugs.

Successive drunks/highs

In this stage, most alcoholics drink daily. Drug addicts, who once used on an irregular basis, now look to get high every day.

Decrease in alcohol/drug tolerance

During the early stages of the disease of addiction, tolerance to alcohol or drugs increases. This increased tolerance can continue for years or even decades. However, the alcoholic and addict will reach a point when their tolerance to drugs and, especially alcohol, will severely decrease, causing them to get drunk or high quicker. During the decrease in tolerance stage, the alcoholic or addict will become sloppy in their drinking and drugging, resulting in fights, accidents, and incarceration.

Hospital/sanitarium

If the alcoholic/addict continues to use, hospitalization for detoxification, or admission into a psychiatric hospital are likely to be needed. For some, detoxification (detox) exposes them to Alcoholics Anonymous and the Twelve Steps for the first time. Although it is rare that anyone gets sober and remains that way after their first detox, at least the seed is planted in the mind of the alcoholic and addict. Some alcoholics and addicts also suffer from mental illness and are referred to as "dually diagnosed." Dual diagnosis complicates recovery from addiction, but does not prevent it from happening. Both illnesses need to be treated at the same time. Some mental illnesses such as bipolar disorder, cause additional problems for recovering alcoholics. Alcoholics who suffer from bipolar disorder, also known as manic depression, are tempted **not** to take their medication, so they can experience the manic feeling which is similar to getting high. It is often difficult to find treatment centers who will accept dually diagnosed addicts, especially if the mental illness has been diagnosed as a psychosis. Clergy may need to reach out to other agencies for guidance in this area.

Indefinable fears

Paranoia and other unsubstantiated fears are common, as the brain is literally being poisoned by alcohol and/or drugs. Addicts will often look out their windows and, even in their closets, to make sure no one is spying on them.

Unable to initiate action, extreme indecisiveness

The addicted person knows that he or she is slowly dying but is unable to take action. Sometimes, it takes someone else, such as a loved one, to initiate the process of getting professional help. Left to his or her own decision making, the alcoholic/addict is like a deer frozen in the headlights of an oncoming car. It is as if as the devil himself has bound them.

All alibis exhausted

The alcoholic/addict is out of excuses. The people closest to the alcoholic/addict will no longer accept the blame, and they will no longer allow themselves to be used and manipulated so that the alcoholic/addict can continue to use.

Unable to work; obsession with drinking/using

The obsession with drinking and drugging will prevent anyone this far into addiction from being responsible enough to maintain a job.

Complete abandonment . . .an "I don't care" attitude

When an alcoholic or addict reaches this very dangerous state, the risk of suicide increases. Every effort to quit has failed and his or her entire life feels like a failure. If a priest is made aware of an alcoholic or addict in this state, it is imperative that he intervenes immediately. A suicide safety plan is laid out in the appendix of this book.

Continued deterioration

The end is near, and everything around them is falling apart. Homelessness, prostitution, and starvation are all possible. Physical ailments bring alcoholics or addicts to the brink of death.

End result: death, institutions, or recovery

All things must come to an end. The alcoholic/addict will either get sober, end up in a psychiatric institution, or die.

These stages are not rigid and do not always progress in the order presented. Neither is it necessary for the diseased person to experience all of the consequences before they decide to get help. Many alcoholics and addicts recover from their disease after only hitting one or two of the early stage descriptions.

Hitting rock bottom is different for everyone, but often, one of four patterns emerges:

There is the physical rock-bottom where the body begins to break down from constant abuse. This results in serious illnesses.

There is the emotional rock-bottom, often resulting from the pain of the deterioration of family, the loss of friends, and the terrible isolation that comes with alcoholism/addiction.

There is a financial rock-bottom, which some reach as a result of job loss or asset loss. This can result in homelessness.

Finally, there is a spiritual rock-bottom, which comes as a result of a person realizing that they are dying spiritually. This is the result of the alcoholic's and addict's awareness that they have truly distorted the image and likeness of God in themselves.

So while the above list is detailed and exhaustive, and includes the physical, emotional and the financial consequences of addictive behavior, it lacks the description of the deterioration of the person's soul while in the grips of alcoholism and addiction. Following is a list of what I consider to be the spiritual stages of the disease of alcoholism/addiction.

Spiritual Stages

Withdrawal from organized Church and related functions

Alcoholics and addicts, who at one point or another were active in their local Church, will inevitably withdraw from church functions and ministries. First, alcohol is usually not present at church functions, and alcoholics do not feel comfortable if there is no alcohol present in social events they attend. Second, most alcoholics and addicts who were once active in the Church, and know that they can no longer control their drinking, will gradually or abruptly stop attending church functions to avoid embarrassing themselves, or be the subject of gossip.

Blaming God for their problems and consequences

Many alcoholics and addicts who were never active at church, or had a bad experience with organized religion, may blame God for their predicament. *"Why is God doing this to me?"* God is seen as a punishing, judgmental God who enjoys watching people suffer. It is similar to the remarks that Christ Himself heard on the Cross. *"If you are really the Christ, save yourself and us."* Instead, they might say, *"If you are really God, help me stop drinking." "If God is the author of all things, then He must be responsible for this."* The alcoholic and addict are unable or unwilling to accept that we live in a fallen world or that we have free will to get sober or to stay addicted.

Realizing they are going to hell

As the disease progresses, many alcoholics and addicts who were once active in the church, or at least those who still believe in heaven and hell, might come to the realization that their actions are leading them to a slow death. This premature death will come at the worst possible time in their lives—a time during which their soul is suffering and they are making bad decisions. Understanding that after death the soul will experience some type of judgment, they fear the worst—they are dying, they cannot seem to do anything about it, and they are going to spend all eternity in hell.

This can be a dangerous time in the life of the alcoholic and addict. With the inability to stop using, and prospects of life eternal in "the other place" imminent, the alcoholic and addict might give up all together and take his/her own life. Clergy must be aware of the red flags and respond swiftly, ensuring that they receive the proper care, while convincing them that they are not evil, just sick.

Foxhole prayer

In the latter stages of addiction and alcoholism, the addicted person will find himself/herself in precarious positions. He/she might be pulled over for a DUI, suffer a severe health crisis, or survive a violent accident. In the middle of these moments of crisis, and as the alcoholic/addict is about to suffer terrible consequences as a result of his or her actions, a "foxhole prayer" might be said. It might sound something like this: *"Lord, if you only get me through this, I promise I will never touch another drink or drug."* For others, these moments of crisis bring relief. Even though there will be severe consequences, it is finally going to be over—*"I'm going to be arrested, or hospitalized, and everyone around me is finally going to find out just how much of an addict/alcoholic I am."* For some, recovery can begin only when "the jig is up."

Foxhole prayers aren't only spoken when an alcoholic or addict is about to be arrested or hospitalized. A person I worked with began to say foxhole prayers about two months before he got sober. In an attempt to help him, his mother took a six-hour train ride to see an Orthodox priest who had special healing powers. She came home with a cross, holy water and a book filled with many of his healings. He began wearing the cross and reading this book. It was at this point that he began to realize that he was hitting a spiritual bottom. He knew that God loved him, but he also knew he was throwing his life away. Every night as he came home at four, five, six, and even seven in the morning from drinking and drugging all night, he would pray this prayer: "Lord, help me to stop living like this, but don't let me get arrested and don't let me have a heart attack." Since he drove drunk often, he had a fear of getting a DUI. He did not want to bring further shame to his family. He thought for sure that one day he would have a heart attack, since he often felt like his heart was coming out of his chest every time he snorted a large quantity of cocaine.

Much like the Prodigal Son who "came to himself," so did this person. One evening, he decided that he had enough. With the help of a good friend, he began calling treatment centers. Two days later he was on the road to sobriety. It wasn't until the end of the first week of treatment that he realized that God answered his prayers just as he prayed them—he got help without being arrested or having a heart attack.

Sometimes, clergy hear foxhole prayers from alcoholics and addicts. Nothing is more important at that time than to help the alcoholic/addict get professional help. The window of willingness opens for only a short time and, once it closes, it might never open again. At these moments, clergy must immediately come to the aid of an addicted person, whose soul is dying and is making one last plea for help.

Biological Effects
of Alcoholism and Drug Addiction

The physiological consequences of alcoholism and drug addiction have been well-documented. The liver is involved with filtering everything digested by the body—especially poisons ingested. Alcohol is treated as a poison by the liver. Continuous abuse of alcohol and drugs damage the liver and kidneys, resulting in the swelling of the organs, cirrhosis of the liver, and kidney failure. A single intense drinking binge can result in death from alcohol blood poisoning.

The organ affected the most by alcohol and drug addiction, however, is not the liver or the kidneys, but the brain. Scientists have known for years that the brains of alcoholics weigh less than the brains of non-alcoholics. Cat-scans and pet-scans can show the devastating effects of alcohol and drug abuse in active alcoholics and addicts.

Recent medical research and technology have pinpointed the neurological changes that occur to the brain when alcohol and drugs are abused. In the March 2004 issue of *Scientific America*, Eric J. Nestler and Robert C. Malenka report on the changes in the structure and function of the brain due to chronic drug use:

Chronic use of addictive substances can change the behavior of a key part of the brain's reward circuit: the pathway extending from the dopamine-producing nerve cells (neurons) of the ventral tegmental area (VTA) to dopamine-sensitive cells in the nucleus accumbens. Those changes, induced in part by molecular actions, contribute significantly to the tolerance, dependence, and craving that fuel repeated drug use and lead to relapses even after long periods of abstention.

Drugs of abuse—cocaine, alcohol, opiates, amphetamine—all commandeer the brain's natural reward circuitry. Stimulation of this pathway reinforces behaviors, ensuring that whatever you just did, you'll want to do again. Repeated exposure to these drugs induces long-lasting adaptations in brain's chemistry and architecture, altering how individual neurons in the brain's reward pathways process information and interact with one another.[54]

These changes and damages can last for a week, a month, or years after the last "fix." The damages of alcohol and drug abuse can cripple the brain. Research shows a genetic pre-disposition to excessive-compulsive behavior. This newer research shows the difficulty of trying to maintain early sobriety, especially since the brain is telling the addicted person that he or she needs more drugs to function "normally." These scientific studies support the disease model of alcoholism and addiction and refute the notion that stopping is a matter of will power.

---

54   Eric J. Nestler and Robert C. Malenka, *"The Addicted Brain,"* Scientific America, March 2004, 80.

Characteristics of Withdrawal

Alcohol is one of the hardest and most dangerous drugs from which to detoxify. The process can kill a person. The person who has shakes, tremors, and other side effects from alcohol withdrawal must be supervised in a hospital environment. Years ago, alcoholics would regularly be arrested for public intoxication. Police officers wondered why many of the alcoholics arrested the previous evening were found dead the next morning. Today, police officers are more aware of the symptoms and the dangers of alcohol detoxification and place many alcoholics in detox centers rather than jail.

When an alcoholic comes to a priest asking for help, it is imperative that he refer the person to a treatment center or, at the very least, the detoxification center at the local area hospital. Recent scientific studies clearly show the need for professional assistance with detoxification. Clergy need to become more inspired and more active in ministry to alcoholics and addicts. However, there are some members of the clergy, as evidenced in the survey, who do not believe that alcoholism/addiction is a disease, and who might simply read a prayer over the alcoholic/addict, and then tell them to go home and detox themselves. While we, as clergy, are responsible for the spiritual welfare of our parishioners, we should also make sure they get the appropriate medical care. The medical professionals should care for them in the beginning, and we should visit them during their detoxification and treatment. When they are released, we should be part of the recovery team or system.

Effects on the Individual and Family

Alcoholism was once thought to be a moral weakness that affects individuals. When alcoholics began to share their experiences with others, they realized that they are not the only ones to face the struggles, feelings, and consequences of drinking. As early as the 1940's, the family members of those closest to the alcoholic began to realize that they shared much of the same struggles, stories and frustration. As a result, Al-Anon, the 12 step program for family members of alcoholics and addicts, was created. In the late 1960's and early 1970's, the professionals at treatment centers realized that the effects of alcoholism and addiction went beyond the individual and had long-reaching implications for the family. Family members, just like the alcoholic themselves, had become sick as a result of living with the alcoholic, and they were also in need of recovery. Our interactions with our family influence our lives, even in adulthood. We seek approval from our families. We look to our families for support, love and nurturing. Whether we live alone or with our families, our relationship with family members can have positive and negative effects on us. Negative interactions are common when a member of the family is addicted to alcohol or drugs. The addict's behavior and demands upon his or her family affect them profoundly.

Interactions with family members may become unhealthy when we feel obligated to do certain things for others in the family, and we feel we have no freedom of choice. We may be told to feel a certain way regarding family circumstances or individuals, when we really don't feel that way. We may be put in situations where we are confronted with the unacceptable behaviors of others in our family, but we do not wish to put up with those behaviors. Interactions with family members are healthy when we make choices that are right for us, regardless of how our families feel about them. We can learn to detach from their actions and behaviors without feeling obligated to become enmeshed in them. We can accept the limitations of each family member, without trying to change them.[55]

Unfortunately, most families dealing with one of its members in full blown addiction do not know how to deal with unacceptable demands put upon them by addicts, nor can they successfully avoid becoming enmeshed in them. As an active addict's behavior becomes more evident, the problem becomes central to the life of the family. As family members struggle to cope, they can become bound up in destructive and recurring situations—just like the addict. In the same way that the addict suffers, the family may suffer as well—maybe a little at first, but then again, and again, and more again.[56]

Even though the active addict knows that at some level his destructive behavior is affecting his family, alcohol and or drugs will eventually become more important than family. The active addict is often in denial of his drug use and the way it affects his family, and believes that next time it will be different. After losing control time after time, the addict experiences failure. This repeated failure destroys their spirit. As this happens over and over again, something dies within the person.

This pattern is similar for family members and the friends of addicts. As an addict becomes more and more dependent on alcohol and drugs, family and friends become forced to cope with the situation. They anticipate trouble before anything even happens. They manage to tolerate the addict somehow because every episode is a new variation of a game that they have all played over and over again. They all know how much deviant behavior they can handle; they push and give a little as they all try to draw the line right at the edge. Families dealing with alcoholism and addiction have to focus too much of their attention on the identified problem person and other family members are neglected.

55 Amy E. Dean, *What is Normal: Family Relationships* (Center City: Hazelden, 1988), 1-2.

56 Terence Williams and Harold A. Swift, *Free to Care: Recovery for the Whole Family* (Center City: Hazelden, 1992), 4.

"The addict becomes a figure like the eight-hundred-pound gorilla that sleeps wherever he wants to. The addict is like the problem child who keeps the family walking on eggshells as they try to anticipate the next outrage that's in store for them . . .When each destructive cycle ends, the family members regroup in an effort to absorb whatever harmful consequences they have suffered. They know in their hearts that they can't change the addict. Maybe it's to soften the truth that families seem to develop their own complex systems of self-deception. They tell themselves that they can help, that they can remedy the situation, if they just try hard enough. They convince themselves that if they just hold on things will be different – next time."[57]

---

57   Ibid.,4-5.

Detaching With Love

Al-Anon, the sister support system to Alcoholics Anonymous, which focuses on recovery for the family of the alcoholic, tells its members that they must "detach with love." Detaching with love is not necessarily "tough love," but a way of coping with the addiction by detaching from the problem, not the person. By detaching, family members are able to love the person while at the same time rejecting their use of alcohol and drugs and the behavior that derives from using. Addiction affects the entire family, whether or not other family members use alcohol and/or drugs. At times, family members may turn to alcohol and/or drugs to cope with the stress of living with an alcoholic or addict.

Family members who live with the stress of active alcoholics and addicts often suffer numerous ailments:

Physically: Stress can manifest itself in health problems such as headaches and high blood pressure;

Emotionally: Feelings of anger, resentment, guilt or depression;

Socially: By alienating oneself from the rest of society or by being aggressive or controlling;

Intellectually: Having difficulty in concentration;

Spiritually: By living a life of despair, disbelief and hopelessness.

With practice and with support from Al-Anon members, family members come to understand that detachment from the dependent person's problems does not mean that they stop caring about this person. Detachment is a way to be respectful of both themselves and the chemically dependent person. The result is well worth the effort of overcoming the obstacles in the beginning. Ultimately detaching with love frees family members to grow to "Live and let live. Let go and let God."[58]

By detaching, the family members begin to take responsibility for their own behavior. They cease to blame their loved ones for how they feel. They begin to understand that the

---

58   Carolyn. W. *Detaching with Love* (Center City: Hazelden, 1994), 2.

cause of their pain is not what others **do** to them. Instead, it is how they **react** to their loved one's behavior. Family members often lose themselves by becoming too involved in the addict's behavior. By detaching, it is possible to regain their self-esteem and self-respect. Acceptance is paramount in detachment. Acceptance does not necessarily mean that family members are fine with what has happened in the past. "It means that they stop trying to change what they have no power over, and they have no power over an alcoholic and addict."[59]

Most know the classical biblical story of Jonah and the whale. But few know the story of what happened to Jonah after the whale. After initially running away, Jonah finally heeds God's call, and delivers His message of repentance to the kingdom of Nineveh. Shocked, he sees the king lead his people in complete repentance before the Lord. Putting on ashes, he leads all his subjects into acts of repentance and a changing of their ways. What is ironic is that Jonah, revealing his ego, becomes angry at God. Then God responds to the people's repentance by relenting, and forgiving them. Again Jonah, egotistically, is angered because he feels like he has been made to look foolish. God responds to him in a priceless way—He asks Jonah a very simple question: "Do you do well to be angry?"

This story communicates an unalterable truth: when we are faced with anything we cannot control, like the actions or decision of a loved one, why on earth would we ever lose control over it, get anxious over it? What is the purpose of wasting negative energy over something that we cannot control and is beyond us? God said it best: we don't do well to be angry. Not only does this question help us to realize and understand our place in the world, our place in the matter of things, it also shows us what our place isn't. It isn't about our egos. It's about understanding our place in the world.

To more effectively deal with the alcoholic or addict, family members should be reminded that detaching with love is easier when they become familiar with the three C's: **Cause, Control and Cure.**

---

59   Ibid., 3.

First, they did not **cause** the problem. Alcoholism is a disease. Family members did not force or make their loved one an alcoholic or addict.

Second, they cannot **control** it. Despite every effort, family members cannot control someone else's drinking or drug use. All they can control is their own reaction to the situation.

Third, they cannot **cure** their loved one. Addiction and alcoholism cannot be cured, but only arrested one day at a time.

Just like alcoholics and addicts, family members need to know that they are not the only people who go through the struggle and the pain that comes when a member of their family is an active addict. Family programs at treatment centers introduce this concept to the families and this helps them to develop relationships with other families who are going through similar crises.

Characteristics of the Stages of Recovery

As odd as it might sound, **relapse** is one of the most common characteristics of recovery. A person who begins their journey in recovery will more than likely relapse. **Relapse** is the most painful aspect of recovery for the individual and often more painful for family members who usually make tremendous sacrifices to get their loved ones into treatment. Most family members do not realize that entrance into the first treatment center is only the beginning of a process which will last a lifetime.

No one is ever "cured" from alcoholism or addiction; they are treatable, not curable. Alcoholics and addicts live life "One Day at a Time," and only have a daily reprieve from their disease, contingent on their spiritual condition. There are some alcoholics and addicts that can get sober without entering into a treatment center. Whether or not they enter a treatment center, the chances of getting and staying sober are best if they go through the twelve-step program of Alcoholics Anonymous or some other related twelve-step program.

Alcohol and drugs are only the symptoms; the true problem lies with the individual. The twelve-step programs not only provide the support and fellowship which are necessary for recovery, but through working the twelve steps, the alcoholic/ addict experiences a change, which can only be seen as a "spiritual transformation." Alcoholics Anonymous and the twelve steps are a program of spiritual recovery. Even the Big Book of *Alcoholics Anonymous* states: "We are willing to grow along spiritual lines. The principles we have set down are guides to progress. We claim spiritual progress rather than spiritual perfections."[60]

Some alcoholics and addicts are able to stop using without AA and without working the steps. Many of them are referred to as "dry drunks" because they still retain many of the negative and dysfunctional characteristics of alcoholics and addicts. Dry drunks are in need of a spiritual transformation which is possible by working the steps and going to AA. Without this spiritual

---

60   *Alcoholics Anonymous* (New York: Alcoholics Anonymous World Services, 1976), 60.

transformation, which is enhanced by being involved in the life of the Church, dry drunks will drink again. This is what I call "mere sobriety," which lacks "spiritual sobriety."

When a parishioner is recovering from substance abuse and working the Twelve-Steps, he or she usually embarks on a spiritual journey; this must occur to reach true sobriety. If the parish priest is absent during this process of spiritual development, it will be detrimental to the recovering person and will reduce the chances of the recovering person returning to the life of the Church. What follows is a list of the twelve steps, a corresponding Bible verse, and a brief explanation of each step.

A Closer Look at Each Step

Step 1.
We admitted that we were powerless over alcohol—
that our lives had become unmanageable.

I know nothing good lives in me,
that is, in my sinful nature.
For I have the desire to do what is good,
but I cannot carry it out.

—Romans 7:18

"Who cares to admit complete defeat? Practically no one, of course. Every natural instinct cries out against the idea of personal powerlessness."[61] The first step is about acceptance. This step has two aspects. First, there is an admission of powerlessness over alcohol or other mind-altering substances. Even a pure alcoholic cannot use drugs safely, other than, of course, those prescribed by a doctor—and even prescriptions can be abused if not used as directed. If this happens, the alcoholic or addict in recovery will eventually drink again, or become addicted to other drugs. Similarly, a drug addict, even one who never drank, cannot drink safely. Sometimes, other mind-altering substances act as triggers which bring the addicted person back to his or her drug of choice, including alcohol. Powerlessness means loss of control; it means the alcoholic or addict cannot control how much they drink or drug.

"Unmanageability" is the second part of this step. It exposes the reality that, as a result of continued substance abuse, the alcoholic or addict's life is out of control. The dreams he or she once had are a blurred vision in their rear-view mirror of life. Though they know better and want to get their lives in order, they fail because they cannot stop drinking and drugging.

---

61   *Twelve Steps and Twelve Traditions* (New York: Alcoholics Anonymous World Services, 1989), 21.

Most recovering alcoholics and addicts work the first step during the first week of treatment. "Working a step" entails reading material from several books including The "Big Book" of *Alcoholics Anonymous*, the *Twelve Steps and Twelve Traditions*, and other prescribed books. Many use a workbook as well. The active alcoholic or addict rarely reflects about the damage, the loss of control, or the unmanageability caused by alcohol or drugs. Writing in the workbook forces the recovering person to reflect on the actions and consequences during active addictions. The benefit of recalling past events and their consequences, allows the recovering person to finally acknowledge that there is a problem, and helps them avoid having "euphoric recall" (only remembering the good times).

Finally, if a person relapses, it is a sign that they have not worked the first step correctly. After all, if one is powerless over alcohol/drugs and one's life cannot be managed properly when using, why would one decide to use again? When a relapse occurs, it is important to rework the first step.

Step 2.
(We) Came to believe that a Power
greater than ourselves
could restore us to sanity.

*For it is God who works in you to will and to act
according to his good purpose.*

—Philippians 2:13

This step is about hope. The alcoholic and addict have admitted they are powerless over alcohol and their lives are unmanageable; now what? Courage has been shown in accepting his or her reality. This step introduces hope for a "sane" life.

The alcohol is gone—but the alcoholic is still here. Something has to change or else the alcoholic and addict will begin drinking or drugging again. Step Two is about a process which begins with baby steps. I once told an agnostic person, "If you do not believe, can you at least believe that I believe." The Prodigal Son who has "come to himself" now begins the journey back to his Father. Many newly-recovering people are agnostic—even some who come to church. Step Two begins the journey towards a relationship with God. A person in recovery does not need to have absolute faith in God to complete this step, just the desire to go through a process which will reintroduce the person to God by continuing to work through the steps.

Step Two also deals with the insane life that alcoholics and addicts led. It allows them to reflect on many of the insane actions done under the influence. It reinforces that they were mentally sick, for a well person would not have driven drunk, or sold their baptismal cross for drugs or left the children unattended while they "copped" their drugs. Step Two reminds them that they were insane and that God could restore them to sanity.

Step 3.
(We) Made a decision to turn our will and our lives over to the care of God as we understood Him.

Therefore, I urge you, brothers, in view of God's mercy,
to offer your bodies as living sacrifices,
holy and pleasing to God –
which is your spiritual worship.

—Romans 12:1

Step Three is about faith. This step is one of the most controversial steps in AA. The word "God" scares many people—especially alcoholics and addicts. *"Why should I trust the God who has punished me with this disease?"* Unfortunately, some people in early recovery still have this understanding of God. Unless this changes, they will use again. A sponsor is very helpful with this step, since the sponsor has experienced the ability to trust God. The sponsor can share how it was hard at first to trust something that could not be seen.

In the Big Book of AA, the early-recovering alcoholics realized they were playing God while they were drinking and that, from now on, God was going to be their Director.[62]

When in active addiction, most alcoholics and addicts need to be in control. What they do not realize is that in reality it was their disease that actually controlled them. Still, to be asked for someone or something else to control them is difficult. For some, the AA group or nature itself becomes the higher power, the god of their understanding. And that is fine in the beginning. It is imperative for them to understand that they are not the true God, but that God can and will be there for them, if only they let Him.

Helping people find God is what clergy do. Even though most clergy are not recovering alcoholics and addicts, they can still share something of their personal relationship with Christ, giving numerous examples of how they trusted Him during their lives, and how those experiences, both good and difficult, improved their relationship with Him. Praying for God's will in the recovering person's life, and beginning to discern God's will, can help to free the recovering person of doubt and worry about what to do next.

Step 4.
(We) Made a searching and fearless moral inventory of ourselves.

Let us examine our ways and test them,
and let us return to the Lord.

—Lamentations 3:40

This step is about honesty. Having admitted that there is a problem and believing that God can help, the recovering person is faced with the daunting task of not only looking thoroughly into his/her past, but looking fearlessly deep into his or her soul. This is an act he or she may have never done before. Step Four

62   *Alcoholics Anonymous* (New York: Alcoholics Anonymous World Services, 1976), 63.

is a common practice of Orthodox Christians as they prepare for Holy Confession.

The writing of an autobiography usually helps recovering people detail their lives and produce a list of things they know in their heart were wrong and sinful. As they detail relationships with family, friends, and even enemies, they begin to remember the litany of "transgressions" they committed against others and themselves. This litany will soon become very important in their journey through recovery and the steps. The list is not meant to judge the alcoholic and addict. It is an exercise in honesty. It is an opportunity to go back in time with courage, and detail words, thoughts and deeds.

Alcoholics and addicts need to learn how to be honest again. They have lived their lives, especially the last few years in active addiction, as liars. Honesty is the most important aspect in recovery—recovery presupposes honesty. Therefore, all skeletons are removed from the closet and nothing is hidden any longer. Spiritually speaking, the alcoholic and addict begin an assault on their disease. Addiction, while it is a physiological disease, is at the same time a spiritual malady. With each step, it is as if another demon is being exorcised from the recovering person. During this step, the recovering person begins to look deeply into their soul, removing many diabolical forces. Many recovering people have a hard time completing this step. Sometimes, traumatic events from childhood which were suppressed become expressed and professional help may be needed. Nevertheless, as long as recovering people are willing to be honest and courageous, they will benefit greatly from working this step. Thoroughness is the key to working a good fourth step.

Step 5.
(We) Admitted to God, to ourselves,
and to another human being
the exact nature of our wrongs.

Therefore, confess your sins to each other
and pray for each other
so that you may be healed.

—James 5:16

It is one thing to write on paper the "exact nature of our wrongs," and another thing altogether to share them with another person. Step Five is about reconciliation. This is the step that some alcoholics and addicts do with a priest. As long as the recovering person was thorough in his/her fourth step, the fifth step should go smoothly.

Clergy must remember that, in as much as the fifth step is similar to confession, it normally does not take place in a sacramental context—there is no or little counseling, and there is no prayer of absolution. In no way should penance be given at this point. The fifth step can take place in church, but without the priest being vested—even if the recovering person is Orthodox. What the recovering person needs most is someone that they can trust to share their innermost and often darkest secrets, without judgment or condescension.

Most recovering people conduct a fifth step with their sponsor. Then again, most recovering people do not have a personal relation with their parish priest. The Hazelden Treatment Facility tells its recovering people that:

"The kind of person, then, that we need for a good fifth step is someone who can be trusted and who is respected yet is compassionate, someone who inspires more comfort than fear, someone who is to some degree a friend. Granted, a listener does not necessarily have to be a close friend but should have the reputation for being an accepting listener and a discerning guide."[63]

Steps 6 and 7.
(We) Were entirely ready to have God
remove all these defects of character.

Humble yourselves before the Lord,
and he will lift you up.

—James 4:10

(We) Humbly asked Him to remove our shortcomings.

If we confess our sins, he is faithful and just
and will forgive us our sins and purify us from all
unrighteousness.

—1 John 1:9

Steps Six and Seven are sometimes called the forgotten steps. Most recovering people, who are able to stay sober, work good fourth and fifth steps but, when it comes to step six and seven, they sometimes struggle. Many alcoholics and addicts complain, even after numerous years of recovery, that they still struggle with their defects of character—the things about themselves which they know are not conducive to recovery and salvation.

---

63   Hazelden Foundation. *The Twelve Steps of Alcoholics Anonymous: Interpreted by the Hazelden Foundation.* (Center City: Hazelden, 1993), 64.

Steps Six and Seven are similar to Steps One and Two, in that alcoholics and addicts realize there is a problem, and that they cannot change by themselves—they look to a power greater than themselves—God to help them.

Working these two steps allows the alcoholic and addict to begin removing defects in their characters, which were often the causes of their dysfunction that negatively affected their relationships with others. These shortcomings are often referred to as the "—isms" of alcoholism and addiction.

Alcoholics and addicts who are connected to the sacramental life of the Church, especially those who come to confession on a regular basis, have an easier time with these steps. They have come to believe, understand, and feel the power that God has to remove sins through confession, and feel the grace of forgiveness during or following the prayer of absolution.

Step 8.

(We) Made a list of all persons we had harmed, and became willing to make amends to them all.

Do to others as you would have them do to you.

—Luke 6:31

Step Eight is about the willingness to restore relationships. Having worked through Step Four, compiling all those events in their lives when they hurt others and themselves, they share them with another human being—usually someone they did not hurt. Now this step is telling them, review your list and compile names. Then get ready to approach even the unapproachable, asking for forgiveness and, when possible making restitution. The workbook for the eighth step asks "But why is making amends necessary in the first place?"[64] Many changes have taken place in the life of the recovering person, asking forgiveness from some and giving restitution to others but:

64   William Springborn, *Step 8:Preparing for Change,* (Center City: Hazelden, 1992), 3.

"There is still a pile of wreckage from our past that must be cleared up. We have relationships that are in disarray. We may have gossiped about others, ridiculed them, withdrawn from them, or tried to control their behavior. We may have condemned them, stolen from them, abused them, or discarded them. Perhaps we gave in to our fears and failed to say no to others when our health and dignity depended on it. In short, we have done damage to others and to ourselves. Whatever our actions, we cannot move forward in our recovery until we do whatever we can to set things right. Our power to overcome our addiction is contingent on making amends. We must be willing "to go to any lengths" for our recovery."[65]

"Going to any lengths," may result in rejection, embarrassment, humiliation, and/or incarceration, yet the recovering person must become ready to go to great lengths to make amends.

Step 9.
(We) Made direct amends to such people wherever possible,
except when to do so would injure them or others.

Therefore, if you are offering your gift at the altar
and there remember that your brother
has something against you,
leave your gift there in front of the altar.
First go and be reconciled to your brother;
then come and offer your gift.

—Matthew 5:23-24

This is perhaps the hardest step to complete. The lengths people go to in recovery are best seen in this step. It is a step of humility. After this step, everything will be exposed, no more deep and dark secrets, no more hidden resentments—everything will come to light. After all, this is exactly what Christ asks us to do. Recovering people have gone to employers and told them that they had embezzled. Others have taken money from charities entrusted to them in order to fund their drug use.

65   Ibid., 3-4.

A person I worked with, knowing that when he came to this step, began saving his money. He almost never spent money unnecessarily. He worked overtime every chance he had and scraped and saved. When it was time, he contacted the national head of the charity and set up a meeting with him. He handed him a check for two thousand dollars, the amount that he had stolen, and asked for forgiveness from the director. The director said that he had never seen such courage and honesty from a human being and praised him for "overcoming." Most people are very receptive when a recovering person comes to them asking for forgiveness and/or makes restitution. After all, most people working their ninth step have been sober for the better part of a year or more. Most of the people around them see the positive changes they have made. It makes sense for them to be supportive of the recovering person.

Alcoholics and addicts tend to hurt family members the most. Unfortunately, sometimes family members of the alcoholic or addict have been so hurt and damaged by them that they are unable to receive the attempt to reconcile the past with a forgiving heart. In those situations, once the recovering person asks for forgiveness or tries to make restitution, he or she has done his or her job. Recovering people cannot control how their efforts to make amends are received. The important thing is that the effort is made.

The result of working this step is a freedom that surpasses all understanding. The alcoholic and addict can now truly look forward to a life free and clear of the guilt of the past. They can now begin working the next three "maintenance steps."

Step 10.
(We) Continued to take personal inventory and, when we were wrong, promptly admitted it.

*So, if you think you are standing firm,
be careful that you don't fall.*

—1 Corinthians. 10:12

Together, steps ten through twelve are called maintenance

steps because they are a continual personal and spiritual reflection.

The most productive way to work Step Ten is to make a daily inventory of oneself. At night, the recovering person reflects on the day and writes down those things that he/she did well and those things he/she struggled with. What will happen over time is that the recovering person will see a pattern of behavior forming. This knowledge will help the recovering person make better decisions. Resentments, which are spiritually damaging and can be awful triggers for alcoholics and addicts to relapse, can be avoided through this step. When a mistake or transgression is made, the recovering person is urged to ask for forgiveness immediately, and to grant forgiveness just as quickly. Selfishness, dishonesty, resentment, and fear must be exposed, for they are dangerous to people in recovery.

Step 11.
(We) Sought through prayer and meditation
to improve our conscious contact with God
as we understood Him, praying only for knowledge
of His will for us and the power to carry that out.

Let the word of Christ dwell in you richly.

—Colossians 3:16

Whereas Step Ten preserves and improves our relationships with others, resulting simply in a life lived in God, Step Eleven enhances our relationship with God. However, the eleventh step might bring pain. Anyone who truly seeks out the Will of God will often be confronted with situations that are uncomfortable, difficult and sacrificial. It is sometimes only through these adversities that our faith can be tested and an "attitude of gratitude" implemented in our lives. Step Eleven presumes a recovering person has the humility to know that wherever they are, whatever the challenges they may encounter, they will be okay. For the best place to be is in God's will—even if that place is a place of pain. Every Christian should work this step and many of the others, but a recovering person involved in the life of the Church is helped by the yearly cycle of the Church as well as the sacraments to truly work this step, not only by himself, but through the liturgical life and Christian *praxis* of the Church.

One of the biggest criticisms of AA is that it focuses on solely an individual spiritual journey and seems to dismiss the role of organized religion. Yet, in the Big Book of Alcoholics Anonymous, when discussing step eleven and prayer and meditation, it states: "If we belong to a religious denomination which requires definite morning devotion, we attend to that, also. If not members of religious bodies, we sometimes select and memorize a few set prayers which emphasize the principles we have been discussing. There are many helpful books also. Suggestions about these may be obtained from one's priest, minister, or rabbi. Be quick to see where religious people are right. Make use of what they offer." This quotation may be found on page 87 of AA's Big Book. Here, we have solid evidence that the original members of AA clearly understood the value of staying connected to a worshiping community.

Step 12.
Having had a spiritual awakening as the result of these Steps, we tried to carry this message to others, and to practice these principles in all our affairs.

Brothers, if someone is caught in a sin, you who are spiritual should restore him gently. But watch yourself, or you also may be tempted.

—Galatians 6:1

Having had a spiritual awakening is different than reaching *theosis*. A spiritual awakening means that the recovering person has come back in touch with their soul. It means that the focus is now on things spiritual rather than temporal. This is the product of true repentance, a sort of Saint-Mary-of-Egypt experience. It is a new life lived in the Lord. The true Prodigal Son experience takes place every day in AA through these steps. Recovering alcoholics become new beings, reborn through God's grace and abundant love.

The other part of this step is perhaps what keeps the fellowship of AA growing. Simply put, alcoholics and addicts "cannot keep what they have unless they give it away." The alcoholic and addict have been given a great gift. As broken as they are, they are the most capable people to help other alcoholics and addicts get clean and sober. Recovering alcoholics and addicts have a responsibility to help others achieve sobriety. A perfect program for imperfect people!

There are some Christian-based programs that use the same 12 Steps but they substitute "Jesus Christ" for "God" or "a power greater than ourselves." While these programs are popular, especially in the South, they sometimes prevent the recovering person from opening up completely for fear of judgment. When a recovering person is not completely honest with themselves, relapse will surely occur. I always suggest to those getting sober that they stay within the mainstream AA groups and treatment facilities, since AA groups focus more on a general spirituality rather than the person of Christ. Some in early recovery struggle with a judgmental God. By introducing the concept of a general God and spirituality over organized religion, newcomers have a greater chance of beginning a spiritual journey. The goal, of course, is to eventually bring them to Christ. Having reviewed and interpreted the steps, as part of the knowledge of the disease of alcoholism and addiction, let us look at the third "core competency."

Core Competency 3

Be aware that possible indicators of the disease
may include, among others:
marital conflict, family violence
(physical, emotional, and verbal), suicide, hospitalization,
or encounters with the criminal justice system.

Finding the Disease While Ministering

Parishioners come to clergy with individual and familial issues and seek spiritual guidance for their problems. Clergy are in a privileged position to help families through all crises. Familial problems can be symptomatic of alcoholism or drug addiction. Spousal abuse should be seen as a red flag exposing the possibility of chemical abuse. Even though parishioners come seeking advice for physical, emotional or verbal abuse, the priest must inquire to see if there is any abuse of alcohol or drugs by one or more of the members of the family.

I was once called to a parishioner's home to pray over their college-aged son who the family felt was possessed by some sort of evil spirit. When I arrived, I learned that earlier that day he was confronted by some Evangelical Protestant Christians who tried to proselytize him and they read prayers over his head. His parents thought that they cursed him. I read the prayers of exorcism and "evil eye" over the young man and anointed him with some holy oil. After the prayers, I sat down with him for about an hour. Slowly, as if I was peeling the layers off of an onion, he began to confess that he skipped class that morning and was walking around high after smoking marijuana with other students. The Evangelical Christians saw him in his obvious high state and tried to preach that there was a better way of life. The young man also confessed that he smoked pot almost every day, and used other hallucinogenic drugs on a regular basis. He agreed to tell his parents the truth and he entered into a treatment center the following day.

Crisis moments, such as funerals, are valuable opportunities for clergy to minister to people suspected of having a problem with alcohol or drugs. In general, funerals cause people to reflect on their lives and contemplate their spiritual health. If they were to die today, would they go to Heaven?

In Orthodox Christian funeral services, tradition calls for a memorial luncheon following the funeral. The priest is usually present for the luncheon, saying the prayer to bless the food and offering words of encouragement and comfort to the family. During this memorial luncheon, family members have a special access to the priest. Rarely do they have the opportunity to be with the priest and have his undivided attention. The combination of spiritual contemplation and access to the priest can result in incredible ministry. It is moments like these that the priest can confront, in a non-confrontational way, parishioners he thinks could benefit from early intervention. Clergy are perceived as "more approachable" if they preach about real issues in people's lives. If a priest preaches about alcoholism and addiction, especially in a non-judgmental way, alcoholics and addicts are more likely to open up and share their problem with him.

Clergy must be ready to encounter denial. Most alcoholics and addicts are too embarrassed to admit to their priests that they have a problem with substances—especially in front of their families. Clergy will have to deal with denial and other defense mechanisms, knowing that their parishioner may not admit the problem, but a seed has still been planted.

Statistics do not lie. Prison ministry is synonymous with ministry to the alcoholic and addict. About three quarters of all inmates were either drunk, high, or engaging in behavior that would allow them to get drunk or high, when they committed their crimes. Many prisons, especially those that are minimum security, have programs and some even special cell blocks, for those inmates who are alcoholics or addicts. Any priest active in prison ministry, or who visits people in jail, must be prepared to encounter people with substance abuse problems.

After a semester of prison ministry at seminary, and now sixteen years of parish ministry where I made countless prison visits, I only encountered one person who admitted that he perpetrated the crime for which he was arrested. Yet, I found many inmates who were open to talking about their problems with alcohol or drugs. I also became aware that inmates can still get their hands on alcohol and drugs while in prison. Being in prison does not always mean forced sobriety.

During prison ministry, clergy should bring up the topic of drinking or drugging with the people they are visiting to see if they open up and share about their addictions. When ministering, find out their release date and ask if they feel that they need to go into a treatment center or half-way house. At the very least, have a list of Alcoholics or Narcotics Anonymous meetings in the area and try to attend the first meeting with them. Do not forget to invite him/her to church on Sunday. These steps will go a long way in helping the former inmate take a correct first step.

Core Compentency 4

*Understand that addiction erodes and blocks
religious and spiritual development;
and be able to effectively communicate
the importance of spirituality and the practice of religion
in recovery, using the scripture, traditions, and rituals
of the faith community.*

Reintegrating the Addict
into the Life of the Church

Here is where most Orthodox clergy fail. Orthodoxy has a faith tradition that is rich, not only in liturgy, but also in pastoral theology. Despite this, clergy seem to be so overwhelmed with their tremendous demands that they cannot, or will not, take the extra time to make the increased effort in order to minister to the alcoholic and addict in early recovery. It is the clergy's responsibility to teach active alcoholics and addicts that they are not bad people going to hell, but sick people who need to become well. The sickness, with which they are afflicted, is a bit more spiritually damaging than cancer. Continued drinking and drugging prevents the addicted person from experiencing the full grace of God and, when untreated, leads to spiritual suicide. Although we live in a fallen world, we still have the ability, through God's grace, the sacraments of the Church, and living an ethical and moral life, to transcend our fallenness. Abuse of alcohol, drugs or other substances, prevents us from reaching our potential, and numbering ourselves among the saints.

At this point, it is appropriate to focus upon the greatest and most legitimate criticism of treatment centers and Alcoholics Anonymous. Many of the faithful who get sober through treatment centers and AA reduce or sever their involvement in organized religion. In a survey given to recovering alcoholics, they were asked if they had replaced their religion with AA. Almost fifty percent said they had substituted AA for their church. Why is this?

The first century Christian Church attracted many people as a result of the Church's practice of communal living. There was a real fellowship unlike any other religion or organization at that time. They shared everything and were part of a group living in the fullness of the grace of God. They saw miracles take place regularly. They helped one another. New members went through a period of initiation (catechism). They were welcomed to the faith by more experienced Christians who served as their sponsors and godparents. Even confessions were public events, with no fear of condemnation from the other members of the Church.

Today, Alcoholics Anonymous shares many of the characteristics of the first century Christian Church. Their fellowship is unlike any other. Everyone in the rooms of AA is part of a select group of people who share a common goal—to achieve and maintain sobriety. Public confession is at the very core of their practices. People are urged to discuss issues, pain, shortcomings, and some admit that a relapse has taken place. Members feel comfortable sharing these things because they know that they will not be judged according to their failures. Instead, by sharing struggles, they allow the other members in the room to reach out and help them. Members speak openly about their relationship with God and how they strive to improve it. Many of their spiritual needs are met through their participation in AA. How many churches today support each other the way that members of AA do? Alcoholics Anonymous is a wonderful supplement to participation in the Church. All recovering alcoholics and addicts need is an invitation through their relationship with their priest.

Rev. Dr. Mark Latcovich from Saint Mary's Seminary and Graduate School of Theology in Cleveland, Ohio has written about the spiritual dimension of alcohol and drug dependence. He suggests that clergy can assist individual and family recovery by helping them address the fundamental meaning of their lives and reshape how they think about God by leading them through a process of reconciliation, personal reformation and reintegration into the community. [66]

Alcoholics and addicts in early recovery are thirsty spiritual sponges desiring to absorb any and all spiritual instruction. They are similar to the Canaanite Woman who desired to eat the crumbs from the master's table (Matt 15:21-28). Most of the time, baptized Orthodox Christians who are alcoholics and addicts have severed relationships with the Church. As they restore their lives from the destruction caused by their addictions, it is equally important for them to restore their relationship with Christ and the Church. Again, the 12-Step program worked properly will place them on a spiritual path with their "higher power," but with which God and what church?

I have always invited Orthodox and non-Orthodox recovering alcoholics and addicts to attend catechism classes. I simply tell them that it is an incredible opportunity to learn all about the Orthodox Christian faith and begin a wonderful and new relationship with Christ and the Church. Those who have chosen to attend the ten class sessions always state that they learned a tremendous amount of material about the Church, but more importantly, that they have acquired an intimate and higher quality relationship with God. When we invite recovering people to attend our catechism classes, it begins their restoration with the Church and enhances their relationship with us.

---

66   U.S. Department of Health and Human Services. Substance Abuse and Mental Health Services Administration. 2004. *Core Competencies for Clergy and Other Pastoral Ministers in Addressing Alcohol and Drug Dependence and the Impact on Family Members: Report of an Expert Consensus Panel Meeting February 26-27, 2003, Washington, DC.,5.*

I often have recovering people from other Orthodox churches come to me for spiritual guidance, and even for the sacrament of Confession. My ultimate goal is to help them begin reintegrating into the sacramental life of the Church, and reintroduce them to their parish priest.

The healing ministry of Christ is continued through the sacraments of the Church. As Orthodox Christians, the sacrament of Communion consists of the priest taking bread and wine, offering them to God and then asking the Holy Spirit to come down and change the bread and wine into the real Body and Blood of Christ. How do the gifts change and what are they changed to? These questions have been wrestled with from the time of the Reformation. The Orthodox response to the other Christian churches was simple: the bread and wine turn into the Body and Blood of Christ *mysteriously*.

The Orthodox Church did not enter into the dialogue of whether or not the Eucharistic change came through *consubstantiation* or *transubstantiation*, or any other theological explanation. The Greek word sacrament is μυστήριον, which literally means "mystery." No one can deny that the chemical composition of alcohol still remains even after the gifts have been consecrated. Yet, the elements have been mystically changed into the real presence of the Body and Blood of Christ. Here lies the dilemma for the recovering Orthodox Christian and his/her priest: should they receive Holy Communion from the chalice and, if so, when?

The beginning of the first step of Alcoholics Anonymous states that *"We were powerless over alcohol . . . ."* Why would someone, who is powerless over something, introduce it into their bodies? And if there are no ill effects as a result, does that mean that the alcoholic is no longer powerless?

One of the young men who I counseled testified to the following. "Two months after I got sober, I was living in a half-way-house in another state. I took a trip back home to visit my family, and on Sunday I attended the Greek Orthodox Church. I came up to receive communion, gratefully consumed the gifts, received a piece of *antidoron* (blessed bread), and stayed to the end of the service. After I returned to the half-way-house and, while I shared in one of the group sessions, I mentioned that I received Holy Communion. The therapist immediately questioned me asking, 'How could you receive communion, which contains alcohol, if you have admitted that you are powerless over alcohol?' I did not know how to answer, after all, no one told me that I could not receive communion. The therapist asked me a second question: 'How did you feel after you received communion?' I answered, 'I felt like I just received the Body and Blood of Christ." The young man had no desire to drink alcohol, because he knew that it was not alcohol he consumed, but the real Body and Blood of Christ.

For many who are in early recovery, it is imperative that they understand that they are truly powerless over alcohol. Therefore, it is best if they wait for a period of time, at least one year before they receive communion from the regular chalice. That does not mean that they should not receive communion. Every priest has a communion kit for hospital visits, and every church has the consecrated lamb on the altar in the *artoforion* (the vessel which contains Holy Communion). These consecrated gifts are used to commune the faithful who, for one reason or another, cannot come to Church. Alcoholism and drug addiction are diseases and those afflicted with them are ill. Thus, it has been my practice to ask the recovering person to come to the Divine Liturgy, pray with the rest of the congregation and, after the blessed bread has been given to everyone and the church has emptied out, to give the recovering person a piece of the pre-sanctified gifts in a spoon, filled with holy water or even grape juice. Since the wine (Blood) has evaporated, there is no longer any alcohol content. In this way, the person in early recovery can receive communion, participate in the worship of the Church and avoid consuming anything that contains alcohol.

We know that the body and blood of Christ cannot hurt a person who receives it with faith. This has been shown historically during plagues, and even more recently during the AIDS epidemic. There is no evidence that any disease has ever been communicated through the chalice. But until the person in early recovery truly understands that he/she will be receiving the Body and Blood of Christ, and that it cannot hurt him/her, it is best to wait. Spiritual maturity in recovery will insure that recovering people will be able to discern that, even though they are able to receive communion, and there is alcohol in it, they are still powerless over alcohol or drugs. I have worked with some alcoholics and addicts who have the necessary spiritual maturity to receive Holy Communion from the Chalice, only months into recovery. For they truly know they are receiving the Body and Blood of Christ. Even today, I know of Orthodox Christian priests who are recovering alcoholics and addicts and are able to consume entire chalices without the desire to relapse.

Finally, there is a confusion of sorts in AA about the relationship of religion to spirituality. In the rooms of AA, you might hear statements such as, *"Religion is for those who are scared of going to hell. Spirituality is for those who have already been there."* Unfortunately, this analogy presents spirituality as being better than religion. When in reality, spirituality without relationship and application of the relationship is not spirituality at all. Since some alcoholics and addicts had bad experiences with organized religion—perhaps a nun who physically punished her students, a priest who seemed judgmental, or the fact that no one from the Church could or would help them during their addictions—many recovering people see organized religion only for its external shortcomings. When one attends an AA meeting, one might hear someone say that not only are they a recovering alcoholic and addict, but also a "recovering Catholic." The *Clinician's Guide to Spirituality* presents the difference in this way: "Religions are a system of beliefs and behavior that are intended to improve spirituality....Religion is rooted in a vision of ultimate truth. Spirituality is rooted in experience. Organized religion and spirituality do not have to be in conflict.[67] Unfortunately, these distinctions are false, Protestantizing, and the marks of American consumerism in religion, where we pick and choose whatever suits us free of commitments and obligations.

I have encountered people in recovery who say they have reached a spiritual ceiling in A.A. And it was only after they connected to a worshipping community that they felt truly spiritually fulfilled.

---

67   Bowen F. White, and John MacDougall, *A Clinician's Guide to Spirituality* (New York: McGraw-Hill, 2001), 16-19.

Core Competency 5

*Be aware of the potential benefits
of early intervention to the addicted person,
the family system and the affected children*

Diagnosing Addiction Early

Early intervention saves lives as well as souls. The earlier an alcoholic or addict begins his or her journey in recovery, the less damage will be done to himself and to his family. Just as early detection of cancer increases the chances of recovery, early intervention also increases the chances of recovery for the alcoholic or addict. More importantly, early intervention increases the chances of the family system staying intact. Divorce is less likely when married persons seek help early in their disease. Early intervention also prevents spouses from becoming co-dependent and allows for a more normal environment in the home. Children benefit the most from early intervention since much of who a person becomes is established as early as six years old. Children need to have a healthy environment, so they can thrive, not just survive at home.

What does this mean for clergy? Clergy must do everything they can to assist alcoholics and addicts in the early stages of addiction, so as to minimize the damage the addicted person does to themselves and their family. This means that we must be proactively aware of the signs of alcoholism and addiction. I have included the model of intervention that clergy may follow, located in the Clergy Handbook section, in the appendix of this book.

Core Competency 6

*Be aware of appropriate pastoral interactions
with the addicted person, the family system,
and the affected children*

Ministry to the Family
of the Alcoholic and Addict

The panel of experts who produced this list consistently commented that clergy should create an atmosphere in which individuals or their family members are encouraged to acknowledge the problem and seek help. Ministry should not be limited to simply referring them to treatment centers, but clergy should ensure that the appropriate support continues to be available by taking an active role in reintegrating the individual and family members into the faith community during the processes of recovery. [68]

Placing someone in a drug/alcohol treatment center is only the beginning of ministry to the alcoholic or addict and their family members. Clergy should engage in a pastoral and sacramental relationship with the alcoholic and addict. In addition to catechism and confession, the priest can begin a regular counseling relationship with the recovering person. This can be helpful if the person in recovery has issues that are primarily spiritual in nature, or too shameful to discuss in AA meetings. Yet, the priest must avoid falling into a codependent relationship with the alcoholic or addict. For example, if the person in early recovery is constantly relapsing, or not working the program honestly, the priest can be used as a scapegoat or crutch, and may be manipulated by the alcoholic or addict. He or she can say to their loved ones that they are trying to get better—that they talk to the priest regularly and that the priest is really trying to help them. When hearing that the priest is involved and communicating regularly with their loved one, family members may overlook a relapse or two, thinking that something has,

---

68   Ibid., 7.

or will change. Without realizing it, the priest has become an enabler to the addict's destructive behavior. Again, the alcoholic or addict has survived for as long as he has in addiction because he was able to take advantage and manipulate people who loved and wanted to help him. There will be a time that even we priests will need to cut-off an addict or alcoholic who is constantly relapsing and not giving recovery his all. To continue helping him might mean that we are enabling him; by cutting him off, we might help him reach the bottom he needs to finally take recovery seriously.

The entire family becomes sick when one member of the family is addicted. All members are in need of spiritual care and guidance. All family members need to know that God loves them and has not abandoned them. Clergy have the opportunity to represent the compassionate Lord. But the priest should not do this alone. He should encourage the family to participate in a family program that most treatment centers provide.

Many treatment centers offer family programs which take place concurrently as the family's loved one is going through treatment. In June of 2005, I spent five days in the family program at the Hazelden Treatment Facility in Minnesota, in a program entitled "Professionals in Residence for Spiritual Caregivers." For five days, I went through the family program with family members who had their loved ones in the 28-day program at Hazelden. What I observed and experienced amazed me. As I heard the pain, frustration, and hope these family members expressed for their loved ones, I realized that they also needed recovery. It was during this family program that I witnessed their healing process.

Since one of the goals of the family program is to introduce Al-Anon to the participants early on, topics dealing with recovery, living with addiction, family issues, and the program of Al-Anon take place before a stress management class and a step class. Presented and elaborated by one of the staff members, family program participants become familiar with the foundation of the twelve-step program of recovery.

To look into the family members' faces was to look into faces of amazement. The information that the family members received was at times revelatory. Comments such as "I never knew that," *"Is that really true?" "So, that's why he did that,"* were often muttered through all the presentations. The environment reminded me of a freshman college classroom at a community college, where people of all ages were intellectually challenged—some for the first time in a while. What they received was very valuable education.

"Alcoholism is a disease."

"My loved one is not simply morally weak, but has an illness."

"The illness is chronic, but there is a way to arrest the problem, one day at a time."

The families learned that they too had become ill. They were given answers to their difficult questions, in addition to the hope that healing might take place in their family. In one of the group therapy sessions that I attended there were three wives who shared the same frustration of living with their respective active alcoholic. They shared stories of broken promises, of public embarrassment, and of constant frustration. They cried together as their stories overlapped. They finished each other's sentences as if they were triplets. Most importantly, they felt like they were no longer alone. The pain and suffering they kept secret and internalized was now exposed. Perhaps most importantly, they felt hope for the first time, hope that their husbands might recover, hope that they too can begin their recovery, and a sort of joy that they could finally commiserate with others who share the same challenge. Every one of the small group sessions I attended included crying, screaming, pain and frustration, but also hope, smiles, and ultimately relief.

Implementation of a Family Program
at the Parish Level

Some of this program can be implemented by a priest within a parish ministry setting. First, the priest should convince family members to attend Al-Anon meetings. The priest should not only have a listing of the local AA meetings, but also of the local Al-Anon meetings. Since most people are hesitant to start new things, it helps if the priest takes them to the first meeting.

Second, the priest can meet with the family members, educating them on the disease of alcoholism, while allowing them a safe environment where they can vent their frustrations, fears, and concerns. I caution priests not to meet more than twice with family members, lest they use family counseling sessions as a replacement for Al-Anon meetings. Ultimately, the goal of the priest is to get the family members into the rooms of Al-Anon where they can develop relationships and fellowship with others, while beginning to work their own programs of recovery. If they are attending regular Al-Anon meetings, the priest may meet with them more regularly to discuss pertinent issues.

If a member of the parish who is in recovery is willing to participate in a Church family program, it will allow the family to truly focus on the disease instead of the alcoholic. It surprises me how some recovering alcoholics are willing to take part in such ministries. I also strongly recommend that as many family members as possible participate in a structured family program at the treatment facility while their loved one is receiving treatment. Whether or not they participate in such a program, I recommend that families meet with me so that I might help them focus on the spiritual aspects of the disease of addiction, become more aware of the spiritual aspect of recovery, and prepare them to receive their loved one, after he or she is released from the inpatient program.

Core Competency 7

*Be able to communicate and sustain
an appropriate level of concern
and messages of hope and caring*

Caring
While Keeping Appropriate Boundaries

It is easy to get sucked into the insanity of addiction. Families will, knowingly and unknowingly, bring clergy into their dysfunction. Clergy must be on guard at all times and be aware of the possibility that they might be manipulated and used. While ministering to an active addict, confirm what he or she is saying to you with his or her family. Addicts will often use the clergy to keep their loved ones off their back for a while: "I'm meeting with the priest every week and I feel that he is slowly helping me." We think that we are helping, when in fact we are enabling them to continue their destructive behavior. Furthermore, marital conflict is a byproduct of active addiction. Spouses may use you to hurt their spouse. Yet, we cannot ignore making some sacrifices to help the addict and his family. To what extremes should clergy go to help somebody?

While I was trying to get a parishioner into a treatment center, I ran into a unique problem. She was a single mother with two children. One of her children was a senior in high school who was able to take care of herself, but the other child was eleven years old and needed to be watched. For the better part of a year, I tried to get the mother into a treatment center. She finally agreed to enter treatment as long as someone could care for her eleven-year-old daughter. With no family within five hundred miles, and no other responsible person willing to look after her daughter, my wife and I decided that we would take the child in for the initial fourteen days of treatment. When the mother finished treatment, her daughter moved back in with her. In another situation, a young man who I had previously tried to help get sober, returned to the Church homeless and asking for help. To test how willing he was to get sober, I asked him to take residence at the Salvation Army until other arrangements could be made. He was willing. For three weeks he lived there, went to meetings, and stayed sober even though many of those who lived with him were drinking and drugging. Finally, I got him into one of the local half-way-houses.

A **half-way-house** is a transitional living environment, where people in recovery live together under the same roof and under rules and guidelines designed to keep them sober. Half-way-houses are used to transition alcoholics and addicts from treatment centers to mainstream life. During the day, residents are urged to work, or look for work. In the evenings, programs and meetings are scheduled to assist the alcoholic and addict in his or her journey through recovery. "House meetings" take place weekly and residents discuss chores, living situations, and receive feedback and encouragement from other residents of the house. If someone is suspected of using alcohol or drugs they are confronted at these meetings. Regular or random drug tests are given. If someone has relapsed, they are asked to leave. Recovering alcoholics and addicts that relapse after treatment or after their initial exposure to Alcoholics Anonymous, sometimes go to half-way-houses. Half-way-houses allow them to be in a more structured environment and surrounded by a supportive community and, for some, away from a dysfunctional homelife.

Normally, treatment programs last only twenty-eight days because most insurance companies do not pay for any more time. Nowadays, most only pay for 14 days, and that is only if you have previously attempted an outpatient program. It usually takes many years for somebody to become a full-blown alcoholic or addict, and somebody cannot be completely cured in twenty-eight days. Half-way-houses allow for some treatment, structure, and accountability to continue, while mainstreaming the recovering person back into society. Half-way-houses also give the recovering person an opportunity to start their recovery in a safer environment, away from the "people, places, and things" they associated with while drinking and drugging.

Some recovering people receive help through **therapeutic communities.** A therapeutic community is an extended-stay facility, somewhere between a treatment center and a half-way-house, which helps alcoholics and addicts that have multiple issues and are in need of severe behavior modification. Sometimes, they can be effective when all other efforts have failed, or for very young people in early recovery.

In both situations that I wrote about before, I had to make some sacrifices—in the first, we took in an eleven-year-old girl; in the second I paid for several months of housing in the half-way house. I caution again: it is easy to get sucked into the dysfunction of alcoholism and drug addiction. Alcoholics and addicts are not immune to using priests. They survive as long as they do because they know how to take advantage of every opportunity and every person around them. On the other hand, when they have a genuine desire to get sober, we must do everything we can to help them. For most alcoholics and addicts, there is a narrow window of willingness to get help. When it closes, it might never open again. Willingness for help occurs when all other options are exhausted, or when the alcoholic and addict hits bottom. It is at these desperate moments that they seek help and are willing to do just about anything to stop using and change their situation.

We must show the appropriate level of concern, expressing hope and caring, and be there for the alcoholic and addict when they reach out for help. Since we are dealing with alcoholism and drug addiction, diseases that are cunning, baffling and powerful, and dealing with sick people who might go to any length to use, clergy must set healthy boundaries which when crossed will mean the end of their involvement with that particular person, until a healthy relationship can be re-established.

Core Competency 8

Be familiar with and utilize available community resources
to ensure a continuum of care for the addicted person,
the family system and the affected children

Knowing How, When, and Where
to Refer Addicts

Knowing where the local treatment center is just the beginning. Some parishioners need immediate detoxification. Knowing the nearest hospital with a detox center allows clergy to get the alcoholic/addict immediate help. Treatment centers are spread out, but most are within driving distance. Some provide such a high quality care or specialty care, that people fly halfway across the country to go to those facilities. Clergy should have a listing of several treatment centers in the area. Once clergy refer a parishioner to a treatment center, they should be sure to inquire about the level and quality of care they are receiving.

Some recovering alcoholics and addicts have emotional and psychological problems that neither AA nor clergy can treat. Therefore, clergy should have a list of a few professional therapists—Christian-based preferably, and well-versed in treating addicts in recovery.

Knowing the listings for the local Alcoholics Anonymous (AA), Narcotics Anonymous (NA), Cocaine Anonymous (CA), Al-Anon, Alateen, and Adult Children of Alcoholics (ACOA) meetings allows for quick referrals and immediate action to take place. Clergy are reminded that family members, including children of alcoholics and addicts, also need to get help. It is vital that they are referred to programs which allow them to look at themselves and address the need for healing and restoration of wholeness. Also, most local governments have social service agencies in place to help the alcoholic and addict get services, many for free or reduced rates. It is recommended that clergy contact their local social service agency for directories and catalogues of services offered.

Finally, clergy must never underestimate the power of God to help people who want to recover by their involvement in the sacramental life of the Church, especially Confession and Communion, thus restoring them to spiritual health. Even AA realizes the awesome power of God to heal.

Core Competency 9

Have a general knowledge of and, where possible,
exposure to the 12-step programs—
AA, NA, Al-Anon, Nar-Anon, Alateen, A.C.O.A., etc.
and other groups

Other Twelve-Step Groups

At many seminaries, students are encouraged to go to an AA meeting to see for themselves what takes place and how this "mysterious" group helps alcoholics get sober. The 12 steps of Alcoholics Anonymous have successfully been utilized by other self-help groups in aiding addicts overcome their problem. **Narcotics Anonymous** (NA) is similar to AA, but the focus is more on drug use. People in NA are primarily drug abusers. Young people usually feel more comfortable in NA because there are more people their age than in AA. Also, since the "pure alcoholic" is becoming less common, and many young people are experimenting with drugs, Narcotics Anonymous is becoming more popular. **Cocaine Anonymous** (CA) focuses on cocaine, drugs, alcohol, all substances of abuse. And in my opinion, it is a more spiritual program than NA and closer to the ethos of AA. Unfortunately, for most clergy, exposure in seminary is the only time they ever step foot into the rooms of NA, CA, or AA.

Al-Anon is extremely beneficial for family members of alcoholics. They work the same 12 Steps, but focus on how they are powerless over their loved one's addiction. They too seek to grow spiritually, and to find a way of living that makes their lives manageable. **Nar-Anon**, the equivalent of Al-Anon, is for those who have family members who are drug addicts. **Alateen** is similar to Alcoholics Anonymous except that its members are teenagers and discussions at meetings focus on the difficulty of staying sober as a teenager. Other twelve-step programs include Heroin Anonymous (HA), Gamblers Anonymous (GA), Sex

Addicts (SAA), Overeaters Anonymous (OA), and countless others. I have personally helped parishioners get into GA, and SAA, and OA, to address addictions to things other than chemicals.

Adult Children of Alcoholics

When is a child not a child? When a child lives with alcoholism.[69] With these words, Janet Geringer Wollititz begins her New York Times Bestseller *Adult Children of Alcoholics.* The effects of alcoholism on children are well-documented. Alcohol and drug abuse, especially in pregnant women, have caused many childhood illnesses including Fetal Alcohol Syndrome, Attention Deficit Disorder and myriad other developmental problems, including mental retardation. In addition to the more evident physiological problems, children who grow up in alcoholic homes will likely have other emotional and developmental issues common in many, if not most, Adult Children of Alcoholics (ACOA). Below is a list of some of the characteristics or generalizations which adult children of alcoholics report during meetings.

Adult children of alcoholics guess at what normal behavior is.

Adult children of alcoholics have difficulty following a project through from beginning to end.

Adult children of alcoholics lie when it would be just as easy to tell the truth.

Adult children of alcoholics judge themselves without mercy.

Adult children of alcoholics have difficulty having fun.

Adult children of alcoholics take themselves too seriously.

Adult children of alcoholics have difficulty with intimate relationships.

Adult children of alcoholics over-react to changes over

---

69   Janet Geringer Wolititz, *Adult Children of Alcoholics.* (Deerfield Beach: Health Communications, Inc., 1983), 3.

which they have no control.

Adult children of alcoholics constantly seek approval and affirmation.

Adult children of alcoholics usually feel that they are different from other people.

Adult children of alcoholics are either super responsible or super irresponsible.

Adult children of alcoholics are extremely loyal, even in the face of evidence that their loyalty is undeserved.

Adult children of alcoholics are impulsive. They tend to lock themselves into a course of action without giving serious consideration to alternative behaviors or possible consequences. This impulsivity leads to confusion, self-loathing and loss of control over their environment. In addition, they spend an excessive amount of energy cleaning up the mess.[70]

In the same way that AA, NA, CA, and Al-Anon have meetings and work the 12-Steps, Adult Children of Alcoholics come together to share their struggles, work their programs and learn how to live life on life's terms. In the course of pastoral counseling, clergy often come across people who grew up in alcoholic homes. Knowing that many of the issues they deal with are common among others who grew up in similar dysfunctional homes is comforting. Even if they do not want to attend an ACOA meeting, Janet Geringer Wolititz's book *Adult Children of Alcoholics* will open their eyes to the cause of their behavior and begin, or improve, the process of healing and recovery.

---

70   Ibid., xxvi-xxvii.

Core Competency 10

Be able to acknowledge and address
values, issues, and attitudes regarding
alcohol and drug use and dependence
in oneself and one's own family

Wounded Healers

During the sacrament of ordination, the ordaining hierarch prays that the Holy Spirit complete that which is lacking in the candidate. Still, clergy are all wounded healers. It is difficult to find a single person, including members of the clergy, who has not experienced some sort of brokenness in their life.

Christian ministers and ordained clergy must learn to acknowledge the authenticity—and thereby the authority—of our own weakness and woundedness, and not our supposed strength; we must accept our brokenness rather than feigning wholeness; we ought to admit our disease rather than pretending to be healthy. Genuine strength, wholeness and health can only come after weakness, brokenness and disease are cured, and to be cured they must be admitted.[71]

Many members of the clergy are affected by alcohol and drug abuse. Whether it was at home as a child, the experience of a relative who had a substance abuse problem, or whether the priest himself has or is struggling with alcohol, drugs or another addiction, clergy must accept that they too have been affected by the abuse of alcohol, drugs or other addictions. The concept of brokenness or woundedness is perceived by many as a negative characteristic. "Yet the idea of a priest as a 'wounded healer,' as a person who—before all else and beyond all else—is aware of his own personal weakness as being the very occasion of divine strength through him, depends and broadens the notion of the

---

71   John Chryssavgis, *Soul Mending: The Art of Spiritual Direction.* (Brookline, Holy Cross Press, 2000). 35

authority of ministry as service or diakoniva. "[72] We live in a fallen world and bear the wounds of that fallenness. "Making one's own wounds a source of healing...does not call for a sharing of superficial personal pains but for a constant willingness to see one's own pain and suffering as rising from the depth of the human condition which all humanity shares."[73] Recovering alcoholics, as wounded as they were and still may be, are the best qualified and most successful in helping other alcoholics get sober—every alcoholic who helps another is a wounded healer. In Saint Paul's Second Letter to the Corinthians, the early Christian missionary shares about a personal struggle, "a thorn in his flesh," and receives a revelation from Christ.

And lest I should be exalted above measure by the abundance of the revelations, a thorn in the flesh was given to me, a messenger of Satan to buffet me, lest I be exalted above measure. Concerning this thing I pleaded with the Lord three times that it might depart from me. And He said to me, "My grace is sufficient for you, for My strength is made perfect in weakness." Therefore most gladly I will rather boast in my infirmities, that the power of Christ may rest upon me. Therefore I take pleasure in infirmities, in reproaches, in needs, in persecutions, in distresses, for Christ's sake. For when I am weak, then I am strong.

(2 Cor. 12:7-10)

Saint Paul understood that to make his wounds a source of healing meant that he could identify with the suffering of this world, allowing Christ's strength to work through his weakness. Recovering alcoholics and addicts also allow Christ's strength to work through their weaknesses, especially when they work with another alcoholic and addict. It is at these moments that Christ's strength is truly made perfect through the recovering person's weaknesses.

---

72   Ibid., 37.

73   Henri Nouwen, *The Wounded Healer: Ministry in Contemporary Society.* (New York: Doubleday, 1972), 90.

Unfortunately, I still run into priests who call alcoholics "drunks" (even at times referring to their brother clergy). Priests must be aware of stereotypes and biases passed on to them or their family members. These stereotypes can prevent them from ministering with all their heart to the alcoholic and addict, and might make themselves unapproachable. Similarly, some of the consequences of alcoholism and drug addiction, especially the negative impact felt by the family caring for the active addict, can cause clergy to direct anger and other unacceptable emotions towards the sick, addicted person. After all, we Christians are taught from childhood to hate the sin, but to love the sinner.

Core Competency 11

Be able to shape, form, and educate
a caring congregation that welcomes and supports
persons and families
affected by alcohol and drug dependence.

Teaching the Congregation About Addictions

The latest surveys show that less than twenty percent of clergy have ever preached a sermon about the dangers of alcohol and drug abuse. Clergy have the ability to shape and mold a community of believers. If priests do not preach about the dangers of alcoholism and addiction, the disease concept, and the hope for recovery, parishioners will not change their preconceived notions of alcoholics and addicts.

Several members of the panel at the gathering that produced these twelve core competencies for clergy reflected on past failures of faith communities, some of which projected the image of the God of "fire and brimstone."

They observed that by heaping shame of threats of God's punishment on those struggling with alcohol and drug dependence or addiction, the religious community—and its congregation—actually may be driving individuals in need and their families away from significant source of comfort, help and hope. Moreover, when it is a member of the clergy who suffers from alcoholism or drug dependence, the unhealthy systemic impact is even more deeply experienced within the organization. One panelist urged the clergy to help substitute messages of hope based on the proven efficacy of treatment, the demonstrated reality of recovery, and the role of spirituality in sustaining recovery for negative attitudes towards alcoholism and drug dependence.[74]

Every congregation has parishioners that are in recovery. Recovering alcoholics and addicts understand that they cannot keep what they have unless they give it away. Recovering people are a tremendous resource in the community. These parishioners are often some of the most active members in the church. They can make up a core group that can help others in the community who are still in active addiction or early recovery. Additionally, they can head up an educational committee on alcohol and drug awareness. **Every parish should have an alcohol and drug abuse Awareness Sunday, held at least once every couple of years.**

The best way to get this group together is by announcing either on Sunday morning, through your weekly bulletin or monthly newsletter, that the priest is seeking anyone who is in recovery to assist with some specific church ministry. If one knows for a fact that one or more people are in recovery, ask them to get others they know from the parish who are also in recovery. This request should get several people in recovery with which clergy can begin.

In Greek culture, which is replete with pride and dignity, sharing one's successes and family's achievements is common. But, sharing the family's problems is taboo. Other cultures are similar. As a result, priests often face a "cult of secrecy," making it difficult to help those who need it the most. Establishing an alcohol and drug abuse awareness group will bring the problem of alcoholism and drug addiction to light by educating the rest of the parishioners on the disease of addiction, the possibility for treatment and recovery. This will expose the "cult of secrecy."

---

74   U.S. Department of Health and Human Services. Substance Abuse and Mental Health Services Administration. 2004. *Core Competencies for Clergy and Other Pastoral Ministers in Addressing Alcohol and Drug Dependence and the Impact on Family Members: Report of an Expert Consensus Panel Meeting February 26-27, 2003, Washington, DC, 6.*

Core Competency 12

*Be aware of how prevention strategies
can benefit the larger community*

Ministry Template

When a program of education for alcohol and drug abuse begins at the parish level, it becomes a model for other communities to follow. Seeds planted through these types of programs produce awareness, prevention, and ministry to all who attend. Such programs can change the perception of others, educate the youth, and treat those afflicted in the world, one parish at a time. It must begin here; it must begin with you.

The Substance Abuse and Mental Health Services Administration (SAMHSA), part of the U.S. Department of Health and Human Services, realized that faith communities could help address the issues of substance abuse and their effects on the family. As they looked at the curricula of various seminaries across the country, they realized that few offered specific instructions on how to work with parishioners struggling with alcohol or drug abuse. They concluded that a clergy training curriculum needed to be developed. This would enable clergy and other pastoral ministers to "break through the wall of silence that surrounds alcohol and drug dependence, and to become involved actively in efforts to combat substance abuse and to mitigate its damaging efforts on families and children."[75]

These core competencies are an outline. I have tried to fill in the blanks by giving you the details on how to learn, implement and refine the core competencies that all clergy should possess for ministry to addicted people and their families—this is your

---

75   U.S. Department of Health and Human Services. Substance Abuse and Mental Health Services Administration. 2004. *Core Competencies for Clergy and Other Pastoral Ministers in Addressing Alcohol and Drug Dependence and the Impact on Family Members: Report of an Expert Consensus Panel Meeting February 26-27, 2003, Washington, DC,* 1.

template. Having expounded on these core competencies, the project will now look at some of the problems or "red flags" which clergy should be aware of in the field of recovery.

Problems in Recovery Today

There are certain "problems" or practices that take place in treatment centers and in 12-Step programs which can be dangerous since they conflict with Scripture and Orthodox Tradition. As stated earlier, treatment centers are of tremendous benefit for alcoholics and addicts, especially for those that are recovering for the first time. They provide a safe place, away from people and places which tempt the addict and alcoholic to continue using alcohol or drugs. They also give the alcoholic and addict a "crash course" in the disease and destruction of addictions. Therefore, the alcoholic and addict have a better chance to stay clean and sober through these programs.

Problems of treatment centers

Unfortunately, there are problems associated with many treatment centers, especially in the last few years. I know for a fact that in 1990, Roman Catholic chaplains would come to many treatment centers on Sunday mornings, and offer a "healing mass" for the residents in the 28-day primary care facilities. Christian songs would be sung, and forgiveness circles and corporal worship would take place. They even had their own chapel.

The Hazelden Treatment Facility in Center City, Minneapolis is one the first and the most respected treatment centers. They have published more material on the topic of addiction than all other treatment centers combined. They even have their own graduate school which produces alcohol and drug counselors. When I attended their "Professional in Residence for Spiritual Caregivers" program, I was astonished to see that millions of dollars were spent on a "meditation room." The walls of the meditation room were sectioned off, and a chair, bench, or kneeling pad was placed inside the partitioned area. People could stare out a window or just stare at a blank wall. In these partitioned areas no one could see each other. The building was purposely built for personal meditation and it was impossible to have communal worship. When I asked the spiritual director why it was built this way, his response was that "worship is a private matter and we wanted to provide an atmosphere where the residents could connect with the God of their understanding." When I asked if there was a chapel in the complex, he said that the meditation center served as the chapel. Moreover, no service whatsoever is offered on the grounds. The problem is that in early treatment newly recovering people are taught that true reconnection with God is a personal act, insinuating, in my opinion, that corporal worship (the worship of an entire community which usually takes place in Church), is not the way, or at least not the best way, to connect with God.

Early Christian monks and writers including Saint Dorotheos of Gaza, express the Christian life in the form of a circle or wheel with spokes. The center of the wheel is God, and humanity lies at the outer edge of the wheel. The closer we move to the center, towards God, the closer we get to each other. The model of the private meditation center represents a very different notion of the God-man relationship. To find God is always also to find other people, not isolation.

Prayer in meetings is another growing problem that I noticed. In the early 1990's, AA meetings would begin with the Serenity Prayer: *God, grant me the serenity to accept the things I cannot change; the courage to change the things I can, and the wisdom to know the difference. Amen."* The meeting always ended with the "Lord's Prayer." During the meeting I attended at Hazelden, a prayer was not said at the beginning of the meeting, and the "Serenity Prayer" was recited at the end. However, instead of saying "Amen" at the end, the universal way of ending any prayer, they recited "so be it." When I asked why they did this, they responded that "Amen" was too religious of a word, and that it offended some.

Problems with relativism in AA

Alcoholics Anonymous was started in 1935, when a doctor and a businessman who were struggling to get sober met in Akron, Ohio. Before this meeting, other groups, including the *Washingtonians,* and *The Oxford Group,* had some success in getting people sober, but the organization had become involved in the political arena which resulted in conflict and separation. Earlier groups and organizations including the *Temperance Movement* (1825-1900) had some success, but temperance soon became abstinence, and their focus was more on eliminating the sale of alcohol than healing people.

It is a well-documented fact that Bill Wilson, one of the two founders of AA, had a spiritual experience one day while he was detoxifying in a hospital. He stopped drinking for six months, but was struggling until he had his first meeting with Dr. Bob, the second member of AA. The rest is history. Alcoholics Anonymous is the most successful "self-help" group ever! It has helped millions upon millions of people get sober throughout the world. The primary text of AA has been translated into most known languages and has sold over forty million copies in the U.S. alone. Hundreds of thousands of meetings take place every year, helping millions of people get sober. Almost all treatment centers use the 12-Step program as their guide, and they refer their clients to AA meetings after they complete their primary programs. However, AA has changed over the years.

There are certain slogans that are often hung on the walls of AA meetings including*: "First things First," "Think, Think, Think," "Easy Does It,"* and *"Live and Let Live."* In the rooms of AA, people are told to accept everyone for who they are without judging them. This is a nice concept, but it can lead to relativism. Everything is relative. What is right is what works for you. Gone are the concepts of absolute truth and dogma. They are replaced with feelings and experiments. I have encountered two people, who, after they got sober, realized that they were homosexual. They had been repressing those feelings all their lives. When they announced this revelation at AA meetings, they were greeted with support. This is not uncommon in the rooms of Alcoholics Anonymous. I asked one of the men who confessed, "What prompted this revelation?" He told me it was something he struggled with all his life and he felt he had the courage, having stopped drinking and drugging and being in such a supportive environment, to "be true to himself."

I told him that "the most natural thing for an alcoholic to do is drink. And yet you do not because you know that it will eventually kill you. And so you carry that cross. Why is it then, if you know that Scripture and your faith tradition tell you that homosexuality is a sin and leads to spiritual death, that you decided to engage in such a way of life? Why can't you see this as another cross which you need to carry?" The liberalism and relativism that allows people of different creeds, faiths, and cultures to come together in one room and share one common goal—to stay sober—is also one of the most dangerous arenas where people can get pulled away from the life and the core teachings of the Church.

In a recent survey, I asked if recovering alcoholics belonged to a church or other congregation before they got sober, and ninety percent said they did. When asked if they currently had a religious affiliation with a church, fifty percent said they did not. Furthermore, almost fifty percent of recovering alcoholics said that they have substituted AA for their church. Is this because AA feeds them spiritually, more than their previous experiences with organized religion? Or is it that the concept of God, "as we understand Him," seems liberating to them?

In the ancient Near East, many worshiped Baal the pagan god. The prophets constantly warned the Ancient Israelites that they were upsetting God through their apostasy. The point is that they still worshiped a "god," a "power greater than themselves," and yet they displeased God. I once had a baptized Orthodox Christian in early recovery who saw herself more as a Buddhist than a Christian. As clergy we have to learn to face frustrations, including frustrations involved with helping newly-recovering alcoholics and addicts. Alcohol and drugs do so much damage to the body and the brain, that it sometimes takes many months, or even several years, for the body and mind to return to normalcy. This demonstrates the need for all clergy to be "hands on" with their parishioners who are in treatment or AA. Alcoholics Anonymous has helped those parishioners when many clergy could not. I thank God every day for this program and the many lives it has saved. Yet, the numerous heresies and pitfalls that abound in AA have to be addressed by clergy, ensuring that the recovering person benefits from the program of recovery while continuing their journey towards salvation in the Church. **The best way to ensure that the Orthodox Christian will return to the sacramental life of the Church is for the priest to be active in the recovery process.**

Appendix

Clergy Handbook Contents

Much of what is included in this handbook that follows, was presented in detail in the previous sections. Below is an outline of the preparations and the interactions that clergy need to practice before and during ministry to the alcoholic and addict.

Preparations

Clergy must be proactive and prepared before a family crisis comes to their attention. Make sure you know where the nearest and most effective treatment/detox centers are available. For information on the nearest treatment facilities, you can go to: http://findtreatment.samhsa.gov.

Have the meeting list of the local Alcoholics Anonymous, Narcotics Anonymous, Cocaine Anonymous, Al-Anon, Alateen, Nar-anon, and ACOA meetings. Nowadays, a simple click on the Internet may provide this information.

Know the various ways an alcoholic and addict can obtain funding for treatment centers. The National Philoptochos can also provide some financial assistance for treatment. Each parish should have a "poor fund" or an "emergency fund," which can be used to assist in offsetting the cost of treatment.

Clergy should attend AA and Al-Anon meetings by themselves, or with members of their congregation, so that they might become more aware of what goes on at meetings and support their parishioners in recovery. Clergy pre-knowledge prevents surprises and any inability to "think of an answer." You will already foresee potential questions and will be prepared with suitable solutions and effective approaches. Prior experience helps prevent missteps in counseling.

Ministry

Awareness of problem/willingness

Family dysfunction, such as children acting out, spousal conflict, police intervention, and mental health issues, can be hints that one or more people in the family is abusing alcohol or drugs. Most of the time, we put all our attention on the symptom (being arrested, suspended, etc.), and rarely do we look at the real problem—addiction. Asking the family members about alcohol and drugs when we minister to them can allow us to pinpoint the problem much earlier.

All ministry begins with the awareness that there is a problem. If the awareness comes from the alcoholic or addict, then willingness to do something about the problem should follow. When meeting with them, clergy should remember not to approach the possible addict in an authoritative way, or as an expert—after all, for some, this is the way they view the Church. I have learned the hard way that initially it is much more effective to interact with the addict in a non-judgmental way, as a good friend would, allowing him or her to do most of the talking. Our goal is to build trust with the addict, allowing him or her to feel that he or she can open up to us and share the truth about his or her addiction. It is also a good idea to change the conversation every once in a while, especially when you feel that you have encountered great resistance, allowing the addict to talk about other things of interest. It has been my experience that, when doing this, the conversation inevitably returns to the topic of addiction. You may need to meet with the addict several times before he or she will consider making the decision to get help. In the course of these meetings, the addict might ask you what they need to do to make a change. At that point, talk about how treatment can save and change his or her life. If possible, allow the addict to talk about what they thought life would be like without the compulsion to use alcohol and drugs. There will be times where you find that the addict's life is in jeopardy as a result of a recent overdose or near-death experience. It is imperative that he or she is convinced to enter treatment. Whether coerced, or by free-will, when the addict is finally willing to get help, the family and the member of the clergy must immediately find a way to get the addict into treatment. The window of willingness opens rarely, and often closes just as fast. If immediate action is not taken, especially after a near-death experience, hospitalization, or revelation, the window of willingness will close, and the addict may never get clean.

This goes back to the point of prior preparation. A good priest needs to have his entire support system set up, even before he identifies a parishioner with a problem. So when the parishioner comes along, the priest is fully capable of enacting a swift process of timely treatment and support.

As mentioned earlier, if the alcoholic is in denial, or is not convinced that he has a problem, these series of questions may prove to be a revelation to him.

Does discussion about excessive drinking annoy you?

Has anyone ever complained about your drinking?

Have you or someone else worried that you drink too much?

Have you ever cut down on your drinking or quit for a while? (Most do not realize that "going on the wagon" is not a sign of control but a symptom of alcoholism. The true social drinker does not play these games of control.)

Have you noticed that you can handle more liquor now than previously? (Again, many will boast about being able to drink more than everybody else, not realizing that elevated tolerance is a classic symptom of alcoholism rather than assurance that one is immune. Only in very late stages of the disease is there a sharp drop in tolerance.)

Do you drink more when under pressure, after a disappointment, or after a quarrel? Do you find yourself making excuses for having a drink? (A social drinker may *enjoy* a drink; the alcoholic *uses* it to cope.)

Do you sometimes drink more than you intend or promise, even though you don't get drunk? (A myth is that the alcoholic gets drunk every time he drinks. However, drinking more than one intends to is a sign that one is beginning to lose control.)

Do you think about your next drink or whether there will be enough to drink?

Do you find yourself ready for the next round of drinks ahead of the others?

Are you sometimes uncomfortable when no liquor is available?

Do you wish to continue drinking after the others have had enough?

Do you do or say things when drinking that you can't remember the next day?

Do you remember the first time you had a drink? (Most of us can't, but the alcoholic often can, and reacts with a smirk, smile or a frown.)

Do you ever enjoy an eye-opener? (a drink the morning after).

Have you ever switched types of liquor to control your drinking?

Does the availability of drink affect your choice of what you do in your recreation time?

(For spouse) Do you see a notable personality change in your spouse after they have had a few drinks?

The person who answers "yes" to two or three of the above questions is probably in the early-stages of alcoholism. Five "yes" answers would be a certain diagnosis, and indicative of at least the early-middle stages of the disease.[76] Clergy should ask these questions directly to the person suspected of alcoholism, with the pretense of "ruling out" that their parishioner is an alcoholic. If the parishioner answers yes to more than three questions, then you should let them know that they are on the verge of becoming an alcoholic. I have seen this information affect several people in profound ways, almost scaring them into not drinking again.

---

76   Wicks, Robert J. & Richard D. Parsons, & Donald Capps, eds. Clinical Handbook of Pastoral Counseling: Volume 1. (Mahwah: Paulist Press, 1985), 505-506.

Intervention

Some alcoholics and addicts that are in the early stages will benefit from being encouraged to answer the questionnaire in this book. If they respond "yes" to the appropriate number of questions, let them know immediately that there is a problem. Others, such as those in denial, need a full intervention by family and friends. If the alcoholic and addict are still drinking or drugging and are not ready to stop, then there is no point in counseling them. The only thing clergy can do is provide an initial meeting where they express the desire to help. Even if parents, spouses and/or children try to do everything they can to get their loved one sober, and ask clergy to do the same, if the active alcoholic or addict does not decide for himself or herself to get sober, sobriety cannot take place.

If the addicted person refuses to meet with the priest and does not want to get any help, there is nothing more that the priest or the family can do other than to implement, and not merely threaten, serious consequences to the addict. This may include calling the police if there is a threat to one's health or safety, or if something has been stolen, or acquiring a restraining order of protection. I have worked with several alcoholics and addicts who tell me that being arrested was a blessing. It took a traumatic experience to motivate them to get help. A loved one may move out of the house, or kick the addict out of the house—especially in the case of a young adult who is abusing drugs. This may necessitate the changing of locks and the arrest of the addict if he or she is trespassing. Refusing visitation of the addict's children may become necessary for their safety, and is also a great tool to show the addict that "you mean business," and that further losses are on the horizon unless something changes. Being arrested, losing visitation rights, getting kicked out of the house, becoming homeless, and the reality of divorce may wake up the addict and get him or her to realize how much is being lost and the consequences of his or her addiction. This realization, and the pain associated with it, is called reaching "rock-bottom." The goal for every family is to help the addict reach this point and realize that help is needed. Unfortunately, sometimes even these consequences are not enough to separate a loved one from the chains of addiction. What is worse, leaving someone homeless or hopeless can backfire and cause the addict to either deliberately or consequently lose their life. This is one of the reasons why families have a difficult time following-up on threats made to the addict—no one wants to live with the guilt that their actions may have caused the demise of a loved one.

The goal of an intervention is to stop the alcoholic or addict from using and to stop any other harmful effects that come as a result of active addiction, which include injury, medical illness, and loss of family and/or work, by getting him into treatment. Denial and unwillingness are the greatest obstacles faced in interventions. The addict has a sophisticated, highly-efficient, and almost impenetrable defense system, which needs to be disrupted by dramatic means. The intervention should be done by people who are significant in the life of the addict. They must be prepared to confront him or her with specific facts concerning the addict's behavior. The intervention should consist of two or more people, with one person in charge, who have witnessed the addict's behavior under the influence, and the consequences of this behavior. Each person must decide what action they will take to impact the addict, unless the addict agrees to enter treatment— an employer might threaten to terminate; a parent, to kick the child out of the house; a loved one, to leave the addicted person.

Some preparation is necessary, including finding a treatment facility with open beds that will take in the addict, checking insurance coverage, finding the funds for treatment, arranging a leave of absence from a job, etc. A rehearsal of the intervention, with all the parties involved to role-play the possible scenarios, is a great idea. If possible, have a mental health professional, such as a counselor or EAP (employment assistance professional), facilitate the intervention. Clergy can also be present for spiritual support and as an affirmation that something must be done. I have led dozens of interventions, but I would suggestion that clergy, who have not been trained in this field, allow a professional to serve as the facilitator. Assure the addict that everyone in the room is here because they love him. Then, the facilitator should ask each person to share incidents they observed while he was high or drunk—and the consequences those actions brought. The addict should be told to wait until each person is done before responding.

The final participant should be the one most influential. This person lets the addict know what is being asked from them—entrance into treatment. Even if the addict does not agree to go into treatment, the consequences that he or she will face will inevitably bring the addict to their knees, causing rock bottom. It is the hope of all involved that this bottom comes before death does. It should be noted that addicts who go into treatment for other people, or as a legal requirement, have a lesser chance of getting sober than those who go in on their own accord and without prodding. It should also be mentioned that the majority of interventions do not succeed in getting loved ones into treatment the first time, but the consequences of the intervention inevitably speed-up their decision to get help. On the other hand, addiction treatment may serve to address denial and open the doors of willingness, allowing growth and change to occur.

Set up detox/treatment
(provide for financial/family needs)

The window of willingness is only open for a short while. Once an alcoholic or addict is willing to get help—**nothing**—including financial issues, should get in the way of treatment. This is why it is important to have access to funds which can make the difference between someone getting help and someone staying sick. Occasionally, treatment centers do not have open beds. That is why clergy should have a list of treatments centers available. If the alcoholic or addict is not in a detox or treatment center, clergy should insist that they attend an AA or NA meeting at least once a day.

Set up special visitations at treatment

Clergy should ask the family, especially the person in treatment, to sign a release form so information on his/her progress can be released to him. Clergy need to know when visits are allowed. Since our busy schedules sometimes do not coincide with visitations hours, clergy should ask if they can visit on other days and times. One visit means a great deal to the addict in treatment. Informed and caring clergy play a prominent role in the ministry they provide to the addict and his or her family, especially if they participate in the recovery program from treatment to integration into the community.

Ministry After Treatment

Ask to be part of aftercare

Treatment is just the beginning of the process. When a recovering alcoholic completes treatment, he/she is given an aftercare program. Part of this program includes going to ninety meetings during the first ninety days of treatment, getting a sponsor, and attending other meetings or therapy as needed. A bi-weekly meeting with the priest will help establish a working ministerial relationship with the recovering person.

Go to AA meetings with them

A wonderful way to bond with the newly-recovering person is to attend a meeting with them. Some clergy might feel a little uncomfortable, but most people in early recovery relish the opportunity to show the priest what takes place during the meeting.

Appropriate Pastoral Interactions with Addicted Persons and Family Members

The pastoral care of an alcoholic or addict can be a challenging, and sometimes frustrating experience. It is easy to feel overwhelmed with the magnitude of the need, the manipulation of the addicted person, and the fear and confusion of the family members. There is a temptation to withdraw and avoid relationships with these people. However, by following certain principles, relating to persons hurt by addiction can be a rewarding ministry.

Try to understand them and avoid irritation or disgust. Addicted persons are used to having others feel disgusted with them, and family members are used to people being critical and impatient with them. If you follow suit, then you are included with all the others who "don't understand." An alcoholic will often use irritation to keep people at a safe distance. Their family members will be more likely to deny the severity of the problem, look for quick fixes, and turn away when confronted with their own role in the family dysfunction.

Expect them to lie, but never accept the lie. Lying is one of the symptoms of the illness. The truth may be painful, but to accept a lie is to deny reality and support the addictive behavior.

Never let them promise you they will quit drinking or taking drugs. Most addicted persons have "quit" a number of times. If he/she promises you that he/she will quit and then does not, his or her guilt may cause him/her to break his/her relationship with you. It is a good rule not to accept such promises and to guide concerned family members not do so, as well.

Do not preach, scold, or tell them they have to join the Church. The alcoholic scolds himself daily and may have had a bad experience in the past with the Church or a priest. You may offer an invitation to attend services but, if you push, you risk pushing them away. The early stages of the relationship are precarious at best. If the addicted person is not attending a 12 step program or group, suggesting and even arranging for that may be more important initially than getting him/her involved in faith activities.

Show genuine interest in them. Addicted persons are very sensitive and will discover quickly how much you care. Your concern may be a stepping stone to finding the concern and love of God and a community of faith. The same is true with the family members.[77]

77   U.S. Department of Health and Human Services. Substance Abuse and Mental Health Services Administration. 2009. *Spiritual Caregiving to Help Addicted Persons and Families: Handbook for Use by Pastoral Counselors in Clergy Education,* Rockville, MD, 18.

Work the Twelve Steps with them

Recovering alcoholics are encouraged to get an AA sponsor. A sponsor is someone who is also in recovery and has been sober for a period of time. He or she has a quality of sobriety which someone new in recovery desires. The sponsor and the newly-recovering person enter into a sort of mentor-student relationship. The sponsor helps the newly-recovering person deal with life's struggles, giving advice and counsel, thereby allowing the person to grow through their experiences—both positive and negative ones—and helping them stay sober. The sponsor is also responsible to work the twelve steps of recovery with the alcoholic or addict. Yet, it is quite possible for clergy to assist in working the steps—or at least helping to interpret them within the life of the Church, especially the fifth step.

Confession—Fifth Step

Clergy are sometimes asked to hear a fifth step from a recovering alcoholic. The Fifth Step is a confession of sorts. After taking a "fearless and moral inventory" of themselves, by truly looking at past behavior including actions, thoughts and feelings, the recovering person writes down all their "sins" and transgressions against God, themselves and others. This list is then communicated to another person, either their sponsor or a member of the clergy. If the recovering person is Orthodox, I listen to the step and tell them to return soon and receive the sacrament of Confession.

Ninth Step

The ninth step is a liberating step for alcoholics and addicts. It is hard enough to take an honest look at oneself, which is done at Step Four; even harder to share that with another human being, which is done at Step Five; but to make direct amends to people one has hurt—well that's nearly impossible for a person who has lived such a sick life and hurt so many. And yet, it is the most cathartic of the twelve steps, and the step that **must** be done if one wishes never to engage in drinking and drugging again. Clergy should counsel family members to receive these amends with love and forgiveness, reminding them that when these acts were done, their loved one was in active addiction and they were not themselves. By the time someone in recovery is working their ninth step, they probably have at least one year of sobriety under their belt, have worked all the previous steps, and are on a wonderful spiritual path. An apology or restitution rarely makes the pain of the past go away. What it does do, is allow recovering people to put past incidents behind them, thereby allowing them to focus on the spiritual journey ahead. Those receiving the amends should not rejoice in that the recovering person acknowledged the hurt he or she caused even though this is important, but they should rejoice that the recovering person has made it this far—a crossroads that, when maneuvered properly, increases the likelihood that the recovering person will stay clean for years to come.

Catechism

I cannot overestimate the importance of asking newly recovering people to participate in catechism, especially if, they are "cradle" Orthodox. Most recovering alcoholics were nominal Christians. Even if they were baptized in the Church, and grew up in the Church, taking catechism classes as adults will benefit them greatly. Alcoholics Anonymous focuses much attention on the spiritual life of the recovering person. They are urged to learn how to grow spiritually closer to God every day. But to which God are they growing closer? AA gives recovering persons the energy, inspiration and motivation to improve their relationship with God. After all, their sobriety depends on it. As recovering people are growing spiritually, they are thirsty to learn everything they can about God. Catechism, when done correctly, reintroduces recovering people to God and the Church, and teaches them that Christ established the Church, and it is in the Church that they encounter the true Risen Lord. Alcoholics Anonymous has a purpose—to help the recovering person stay sober and help others get sober. However, true salvation comes through Jesus Christ. Alcoholic Anonymous saves lives, but the sacramental life which can only be lived in the Church saves souls. For the recovering alcoholic and addict, both are needed to prosper physically and spiritually.

Communion Issue

Orthodox priests should be careful when distributing communion to recovering alcoholics and addicts. Even though the Body and Blood of Christ is meant for forgiveness of sins and life eternal, a newly recovering person should wait before receiving communion from the chalice. It is best to give them communion from the pre-sanctified gifts with a little bit of holy water or grape juice in the spoon given after liturgy. It is always prudent to confer with your local hierarch and receive his blessing before distributing communion in this manner. I have found it best to wait up to a year before distributing communion from the chalice to recovering people. It is not that communion can cause the recovering person harm, but since AA is a program of total abstinence and no amount of alcohol is considered safe, and since communion does have alcohol, even after the consecration, it is best to wait until recovering people are at a place in their spiritual recovery where they understand that it is truly the Body and Blood of Christ that they are receiving and that it cannot hurt them.

A discussion with the recovering person's sponsor, explaining the theology of communion and making him or her aware that you feel that it is time for he or she to receive with everyone else from the chalice is recommended. One may see restricting the recovering person from communion as keeping with certain canonical restrictions that suspend communion while repentance takes place. This restriction is not for the disease of addiction, of course, but for the many sins that likely coincide with life in addiction. Most of the time, recovering alcoholics and addicts are so beat up from trying to survive, that once they get sober and begin their spiritual journeys in recovery, reintegration into the sacramental life of the Church begins quickly. Again, I have yet to see a single alcoholic or addict relapse as a result of receiving communion from the Holy Chalice. Nevertheless, it is prudent to proceed with caution.

Dealing with relapse

One of the least desirable aspects of ministry to alcoholics and addicts is relapse. Since only one out of thirty people exposed to AA, recovery, or treatment recover without ever relapsing, it is something that all clergy and family members have to deal with. Relapse is a process that begins with slight and often unseen changes in thinking attitude and behavior. Relapse occurs when people in recovery stop working their programs. This happens when alcoholics and addicts stop going to meetings, stop working their steps, begin to spend more time with people and in places that were associated with using alcohol and drugs. Over a period of time, sometimes weeks, months or years, attitudes, beliefs, and emotions change to the point where use of mind-altering substances begins again. Once a person reaches this point, it is almost impossible not to use.

The Big Book of Alcoholics Anonymous warns us about what happens when an alcoholic reaches this state: The alcoholic at certain times has no effective mental defense against the first drink. Except in a few rare cases, neither he nor any other human being can provide such a defense. His defense must come from a Higher Power.[78]

When a relapse occurs, do not panic—it does not mean that efforts by clergy and others have failed. Treatments, half-way houses, and meetings have helped educate and keep the alcoholic or addict clean and sober for a period of time. Recovery will most likely begin again—the question is when. Most importantly, alcoholics or addicts must admit that they have relapsed. Afterwards, there must be a desire to get clean and sober again. If they want to begin sobriety again, then clergy should assist them, having helped them understand why they relapsed in the first place.

If there is no desire to get clean and sober, then clergy **must back off**. To help them financially or otherwise would mean enabling them to continue their destructive behavior. When an alcoholic or addict continues to relapse over and over again, there might not be a sincere attempt to get sober or a sincere

78   *Alcoholics Anonymous* (New York: Alcoholics Anonymous World Services, 1976), 43.

desire to get honest. There are times when clergy have to cut off all ties with alcoholics and addicts and let them decide if they really want to live a life free of alcohol or drugs.

Suicide Prevention

Occasionally, when ministering to alcoholics and addicts, or during ministry in general, we encounter parishioners who are suicidal. Some alcoholics and addicts may have attempted suicide at one point or another during their active addiction. Some might have attempted it or wish to attempt suicide out of the frustration of constantly relapsing and not being able to put together any real clean time.

According to the Center for Disease Control (2010), suicide takes the lives of about 38,000 Americans, and about 465,000 people a year are seen in emergency room department for self-injury. Studies have shown that faith communities are a great setting for suicide prevention, since people who are religious have a greater moral objection to suicide. Furthermore, spiritual beliefs and practices help people feel greater hope, connectedness, and find meaning in their lives.

As clergy, we need to be alert concerning the problems that face the members of our community, especially when it is one that is so physically and spiritually destructive. Some of the signs of immediate risk for suicide include: talking about wanting to die or kill oneself, looking for a way to kill oneself, such as searching online, obtaining a gun, talking about feelings of hopelessness, or having no reason to live. The national suicide prevention hotline is 1-800-273-8255. Knowing if there have there been prior suicide attempts, if there is there is any alcohol or drug abuse, if there is a history of mental illnesses or just simply mood or anxiety disorders, will help you determine the seriousness of the suicide threat.

If you are working with somebody who mentions the desire to kill him or herself, you might want to make a safety plan with him or her. Ask them to list the five signs that bring them to bad thoughts. These may include loneliness, isolation, relationships, etc. Then ask them to always pay close attention to these signs and to call someone when they feel that they are consuming them. Then, ask them to list five things that they can do to get out of their bad thinking. These may include calling someone, seeing someone, doing something such as going to a movie, to the gym, or especially going to a meeting if they are already part of a 12-Step program. Finally, ask them again to list places they can go and people that they can see to help them get away from these bad thoughts. Be sure to write down all the people's names and phone numbers on the paper, so they can call them when they are having suicidal thoughts.

Please remember that in this situation, especially if you have no experience with helping others overcome the desire to end their life, it's best to leave it to the professionals. Many States will hold people who are suicidal for a period of 72 hours, so they might make a psychological evaluation. This keeps the person safe for a short period of time, and if necessary, allows the administration of certain psychotropic medications, which might address the core issue of suicidal thoughts and find balance in the chemistry of the brain.

Self-Awareness

Clergy are not invincible. We all deal with issues from our childhood and in our past that might be unresolved. Maybe we grew up in an alcoholic home. Maybe we experimented with excessive drinking or drugs in our adolescence or at some time in our past. Maybe we still do not believe that addiction is a disease, and can simply be controlled by will-power. It is imperative to understand ourselves, and the aspects of our ministries that make us feel vulnerable, and unable to minister effectively.

I have worked with three members of the clergy, who have shared that as they were ministering to an alcoholic in their congregation, they were overtaken by a rush of emotions that seemed to paralyze them. Two of these clergy grew up in alcoholic homes, and the other in an abusive home. All three were not ready for the flood of emotions, which were released as a result of working with an addict.

It is not just experiences in our youth that affect the way we minister. Some clergy have traumatic experiences while ministering. These experiences impact the way they minister in the future. As a newly ordained priest, I was very active in hospital ministry. In one case, a father of five fainted and severely injured his head. I visited him and ministered to the children who ranged in age from seven months to twenty-one years of age. After several days, the neurologists told his wife that there was no brain activity and no hope for recovery. She insisted that I be with her as she told the family this sad news. Two days later, I was praying with the entire family as they took him off the life support. As his vital signs were failing, the mother gave me her seven-month old son and asked that I take his hand and touch his father for the last time. Little did I know how profound an affect this request had on me.

As I was running this baby's hand over his dying father's arm, I started weeping uncontrollably. My tears were not necessarily for the loss of the father, though that was terribly sad. My tears were not even necessarily for this seven-month-old baby who was saying goodbye to his father, never to see him again. No, my tears, I realized afterwards, were coming from the fact that my daughter was also seven months old, and I thought about this scene playing in my own life. What if it was me who was dying and it was my daughter whose hand was touching me for the last time? What if she grew up not knowing me, without my presence in her formidable years, without my presence when she graduated from college, got married, had children? This is what I was thinking. The father eventually fell asleep in the Lord, and I officiated over his funeral. During the next few years, I cried every time I had to visit a child in the hospital. I cried before I visited the child and I cried after I left. I literally dreaded going to the hospital to visit children.

Fifteen years later, I still struggle a bit and have to hold back tears when I visit a child in the hospital. But today, I am aware of why I feel this way—it is a direct result of a moment of great impact, not just in my ministry, but in my life. I was scarred by the experience, and yet every day, and every visit, helps me recover from that traumatic experience. We are taught to open our hearts, to empathize with those to whom we are ministering, and then leave it all behind and be sure never to bring it home. I must confess, when I went home that night, I held my child in my arms for hours. When ministering to alcoholics and addicts, clergy can become caught up in extremely stressful situations. Being aware of all their "scars," (their prior experiences with alcoholism and addiction, as well as any dysfunction in their childhood) will allow clergy to effectively minister without being "blind-sided" by those experiences.

Develop a recovery group

A core of people who are either in recovery, have family members in recovery, or have a considerable amount of knowledge about alcoholism and drug addiction, should meet regularly and plan educational seminars on the dangers of alcohol and drug abuse. They should also be utilized in ministry as people who can help others in the community that are struggling with alcoholism or drug addiction. In this capacity, they can serve as an extended or "Greek Family" helping alcoholics and addicts in their journey towards recovery. Most people think of treatment for alcoholism and drug addiction as the cure for the illness—you go to treatment and you get better—you take your medicine, go to therapy, and become cured. Not so, it is a long-term process. Dr. Thomas McLellan, the director of the Treatment Institute at the University of Pennsylvania, states: "The real work of recovery includes helping an individual reintegrate him or herself in the community, the success of which rests frequently on the availability of community support.[79]

Increasing alcohol and drug awareness in the community

If clergy talk about alcoholism and drug addiction from the pulpit, then parishioners and family members are more likely to approach them with such problems in their homes. Some religions have a limited lectionary from which a member

79   U.S. Department of Health and Human Services. Substance Abuse and Mental Health Services Administration. 2004. *Core Competencies for Clergy and Other Pastoral Ministers in Addressing Alcohol and Drug Dependence and the Impact on Family Members: Report of an Expert Consensus Panel Meeting February 26-27, 2003,* Washington, DC.,4.

of the clergy can preach. Yet, most can find a way to discuss addiction within the context of a particular scriptural reading. A yearly Drug and Alcohol Awareness Sunday is a great way to communicate to your faithful that addiction is a problem and that we are here to help. Sometimes, unfortunate situations can provide a reason to shed the spotlight of awareness. At one of our overnight youth trips, it was revealed that a teenager had brought alcohol and drugs with him. After addressing the issue with the young man and his family, one of my youth workers suggested that we invite someone from AA to speak to all the youth. A young woman came the following week and shared her experience, strength, and hope. I cannot tell you how positively she affected our young people. I remember them talking about her story two years later. Developing a congregation that is aware of addiction promotes a caring community and welcomes those with addictions with love and without judgment.

Remove the Stigma of Addiction

It has been said that "the Church is the hospital for the souls." If this is true, then there are many spiritually sick people in the Church—and that is exactly where they should be. Unfortunately, spiritually sick people often bring their prejudices into the community.

There is a process with stigma that involves a downward spiral for those impacted by alcoholism or substance abuse and contributes to, rather than helps, the damaging addictive behavior. Stigma leads to shame. Shame leads to withdrawal. Withdrawal leads to isolation. Isolation leads to more drinking/drugging and denial of reality, which ultimately leads to hitting bottom. Thus, helping to remove stigma from alcoholism and other addictions is something that religious communities can contribute to ending this vicious cycle and encouraging help at an early stage of addiction for both the afflicted individual and the impacted family members.[80]

---

80   U.S. Department of Health and Human Services. Substance Abuse and Mental Health Services Administration. 2009. Spiritual Caregiving to Help Addicted Persons and Families: *Help Addicted Persons and Families: Handbook for Use by Pastoral Counselors in Clergy Education,* Rockville, MD, 9.

Conclusion

It is my hope that this study will spark conversations about the way in which clergy should minister to alcoholics and addicts. Progress in this field is evident. Twenty years ago, I didn't know of any Greek Orthodox church that allowed AA or other twelve-step recovery groups to meet inside their congregations. Today, there are now about a dozen Greek Orthodox parishes who host weekly AA meetings. In my home parish of Saint Paraskevi in Greenlawn, NY, we house homeless people during the winter months. Since most of the homeless we feed and bed down are of Hispanic background, and since many have a dependency on alcohol, we host a Spanish-speaking AA meeting for them. Sharing these ministries with other clergy might create networks and inspire others to begin similar ministries in their parishes.

What further study is needed?

Most addictions share many of the same characteristics and use similar means for recovery. The scope of this project was limited to those addicted to alcohol and drugs. Addictions to gambling, eating, sex, etc., can be as destructive. Other addictions can be treated in the same way as alcohol and drugs. Studies focusing on other addictions, their specific destructive patterns, and the unique aspects of their recovery would be beneficial. Lastly, the stresses and strains of parish ministry, and the inability to find healthy means of releasing stress, sometimes lead clergy to chemical dependency and often to clergy burn-out. A study focusing on the increased alcoholism and drug addiction among members of the clergy, along with a guide on how to help them get clean and sober is needed.

Index

BIBLIOGRAPHY

Alcoholics Anonymous. New York: Alcoholics Anonymous World Services, 1976.

Alcoholics Anonymous Comes of Age. New York: Alcoholics Anonymous World Services, 1996.

Allen, Joseph J. *The Ministry of the Church: Image of Pastoral Care.* Crestwood: Saint Vladimir's Seminary Press, 1986.

_____. *Inner Way: Toward a Rebirth of Eastern Christian Spiritual Direction.*   Brookline: Holy Cross Orthodox Press, 2000.

_____. ed. *Orthodox Synthesis: The Unity of Theological Thought.* Crestwood: St. Vladimir's Seminary Press, 1981.

Apthorp, Stephen P. *Alcohol and Substance Abuse: A Clergy Handbook.* Wilton: Morehouse-Barlow, 1985

B, Mel. *My Search for Bill W.* Center City: Hazelden, 2000.

Bissell, LeClair & Royce, James E. *Ethics: For Addiction Professionals.* Center City: Hazelden, 1987.

Chapman, Thomas W. *A Practical Handbook for Ministry: From the Writings of Wayne E. Oates.* Westminster/John Knox Press, 1992.

Clinebell, Howard J. *Understanding and Counseling the Alcoholic*, New York: Council Press, 1978, 323.

Chryssavgis, John. *Soul Mending: The Art of Spiritual Direction.* Brookline: Holy Cross Orthodox Press, 2000.

Constantinides, Evagoras. *The Priest's Service Book.* Merrillville; Evagoras Constantinides, 1989.

Dean, Amy E. *What Is Normal?: Family Relationships.* Center City: Hazelden, 1988.

Edwards, John T. *Treating Chemically Dependent Families: A Practical Systems Approach For Professionals.* New York: Johnson Institute, 1990.

Fisher, Gary L. & Harrison, Thomas C. *Second Edition: Substance Abuse: Information for School Counselors, Social Workers, Therapists, and Counselors.* Needham Heights: Allyn & Bacon, 2000.

Geringer Wolititz, Janet. *Adult Children of Alcoholics.* Deerfield Beach: Health Communications, Inc., 1983.

Goggins, Gerald. *The Anonymous Disciple.* Worcester: Ambassador Books, 1995.

_____, ed.. *Father Fred and the Twelve Steps: A primer for Recovery.* Worcester: Ambassador Books, 2001.

Gorski, Terence T. *The Relapse/Recovery Grid.* Center City: Hazelden, 1989.

Hamel, Richard A. *A Good First Step: A First Step Workbook For Twelve Step Programs.* Center City: Hazelden, 1985.

Hazelden Foundation. *Keep It Simple: Working the 12 Steps.* Center City: Hazelden Foundation, 1988.

_____. *The Twelve Steps: A Healing Journey.* Center City: Hazelden, 1986.

_____. *The Twelve Steps Of Alcoholics Anonymous: Interpreted by the Hazelden Foundation.* Center City: Hazelden, 1993.

Helgoe, Robert S. *Hierarchy of Recovery: From Abstinence to Self-Actualization.* Center City: Hazelden, 2002.

Hettelhack, Guy. *First Year Sobriety: When All That Changes Is Everything.* Center City: Hazelden, Minnesota, 1992.

Hoff, Lee Ann. *People in Crisis: Understanding and Healing. Third Edition.* Redwood City: Addison-Wesley Publishing Company, Inc., 1989.

Holst, Lawrence E., ed. *Hospital Ministry: The Role of the Chaplain Today.* New York: Crossroad Publishing, 1996.

Ivey, Allen E. & Ivey, Mary Bradford & Simek-Morgan, Lynn. *Counseling and Psychotherapy: A Multicultural Perspective, Third Edition.*, Needham Heights, MA: Allyn & Bacon, 1993.

Kurtz, Ernest. *Not-God: a History of Alcoholics Anonymous.* Center City: Hazelden, 1979.

May, Gerald, G. *Addiction and Grace: Love and Spirituality in the Healing of Addictions.* San Francisco: Harper San Francisco, 1988.

Merrill, Kraft, Gordon, Holmes & Walker. *Chemically Dependent Older Adults: How Do We Treat Them?* Center City: Hazelden, 1990.

Meyers, Robert J. & Wolfe, Brenda L. *Get Your Loved One Sober: Alternatives to Nagging, Pleading and Threatening.* Center City: Hazelden, 2004.

Mihailoff, Victor. *Breaking the Chains of Addiction: How to Use Ancient Eastern Orthodox Spirituality to Free our Minds and*

Bodies from all Addictions. Salisbury: Regina Orthodox Press, 2005.

Milam, James R. and Katherin Ketchum. *Under the Influence.* Seattle: Madrona Publishers, 1981.

Miller, William R. & Katherine A. Jackson. *Practical Psychology for Pastors, Second Edition.* Englewood Cliffs: Prentice Hall, 1995.

Morgan, Oliver J. & Jordan, Merle, ed. *Addiction and Spirituality: A Multidisciplinary Approach.* Saint Louis: Chalice Press, 1999.

Nakken, Craig. *The Addictive Personality: Understanding the Addictive Process and Compulsive Behavior.* Center City: Hazelden, 1988.

_____*Reclaim Your Family From Addiction: How Couples And Families Recover Love and Meaning.* Center City: Hazelden, 2000.

National Center of Addiction and Substance Abuse at Columbia University entitled *So Help Me God: Substance Abuse, Religion and Spirituality*, November 2001

Nelson, James B. *Thirst: God and the Alcoholic Experience.* Louisville: Westminster/John Knox Press, 2004.

Nestler, Eric J. and Robert C. Malenka. *"The Addicted Brain,"* Scientific America, March, 2004.

Newhouse, Eric. *Alcohol: Cradle to Grave.* Center City: Hazelden, 2001.

Nouwen, Henri. *The Wounded Healer: Ministry in Contemporary Society.* New York: Doubleday, 1972.

Nowinski, Joseph & Stuard Baker. *The Twelve-Step Facilitation Handbook: A Systematic Approach To Recovery From Substance*

Dependence. Center City: Hazelden, 2003.

P. Bill & D. Lisa. *Second Edition: The 12 Step Prayer Book: A Collection of Favorite 12 Step Prayers and Inspirational Readings.* Center City: Hazelden, 2004.

Pfau, Fr. Ralph & Al Hirshberg. *Prodigal Shepherd.* The SMT Guild: Indianapolis, Indiana, 1989.

Pittman, Bill & B., Dick. *Courage To Change: The Christian Roots of The Twelve-Step Movement.* Center City: Hazelden, 1994.

Pruyser, Paul W. *The Minister as Diagnostician: Personal Problems in Pastoral Perspective.* Philadelphia: Harper & Row, 1968.

Purves, Andrew. *The Search for Compassion: Spirituality and Ministry.* Louisville: Westminster/John Knox Press, 1989.

_____. *Pastoral Theology in the Classical Tradition.* Louisville: Westminster/John Knox Press, 2001.

Ringwald, Christopher D. *The Soul of Recovery: Uncovering the Spiritual Dimension of the Treatment of Addictions.* New York: Oxford University Press, 2002.

Roukema, Richard W. *Counseling for the Soul in Distress.* New York: Hawthorn Press, 2003.

Saint Athanasios. *On the Incarnation.*, Crestwood: Saint Vladimir's Orthodox Seminary Press, 2003.

Saint John Chrysostom. *On Wealth and Poverty.* Roth, Catherine P., trans. Crestwood: Saint Vladimir's Seminary Press, 1984.

Schafff, Phillip ed. *Nicene and Post Nicene Fathers* Vol. IVX [CD-ROM] Albany: Ages Software, 1997.

Shelton, Charles M. *Pastoral Counseling With Adolescents and Young Adults.* New York: Crossroad Publishing Company, 1995.

Skibbins, David. *Working Clean and Sober: A Guide For All Recovering People.* Center City: Hazelden, 2000.

Smith, David E. & Donald R. Wesson. *Treating Cocaine Dependency.* Center City: Hazelden Foundation, 1988.

Springborn, William. *Steps 1-12.* Center City: Hazelden Foundation, 1997.

Staniloae, Dimitru. *Orthodox Spirituality.* South Canaan: St, Tikhon's Seminary Press, 2003.

Stylianopoulos, Theodore. *Bread for Life: Reading the Bible.* Brookline: Greek Orthodox Department of Religious Education, 1988.

Twelve Steps and Twelve Traditions (New York: Alcoholics Anonymous World Services, 1989), 21.

The Twelve Steps: A Spiritual Journey: A Working Guide for Healing, Revised Edition. San Diego: RPI Publishing, Inc., 1994.

Turabian, Kate L. *A Manual for Writers of Term Papers, Theses, and Dissertations, Sixth Edition.* Chicago: University of Chicago Press, 1996.

U.S. Department of Health and Human Services. Substance Abuse and Mental Health Services Administration. *Core Competencies for Clergy and Other Pastoral Ministers in Addressing Alcohol and Drug Dependence and the Impact on Family Members: Report of an Expert Consensus Panel Meeting February 26-27, 2003,* Washington, DC., 2004.

U.S. Department of Health and Human Services. Substance Abuse and Mental Health Services Administration. *Spiritual Caregiving to Help Addicted Persons and Families:*

HANDBOOK FOR USE BY PASTORAL COUNSELORS IN CLERGY EDUCATION, Rockville, MD., 2009.

Vlachos, Hierotheos. *Orthodox Psychotherapy: The Science of the Fathers*, Esther Williams, trans. Levadia: Birth of the Theotokos Monastery, 1994.

W. Anne. *Take What Works: How I Made The Most Of My Recovery Program.* Center City: Hazelden Foundation, 1989.

Webber, Meletios. *Steps of Transformation: An Orthodox Priest Explores the Twelve Steps.* Ben Lomond: Conciliar Press, 2003.

White, Bowen, F and John A. Mac Dougall. *Clinician's Guide to Spirituality.* New York: McGraw-Hill, 2001.

Wicks, Robert J. & Richard D. Parsons, & Donald Capps, ed. *Clinical Handbook of Pastoral Counseling: Volume 1.* Mahwah: Paulist Press, 1985.

Williams Terence & Harold A. Swift. *Free to Care: Recovery for the Whole Family.* Center City: Hazelden 1992.

W. Carolyn. *Detaching with Love.* Center City: Hazelden, 1994.